NATURE'S
MEDICINE
FOR THE
TROUBLED
SOUL

THE

HEALING

EARTH

PHILIP SUTTON CHARD

NORTHWORD PRESS
Minnetonka, Minnesota

With heartfelt gratitude to both my mothers:
Pauline Florence Chard
Mother Earth

NorthWord Press
5900 Green Oak Drive
Minnetonka, MN 55343
1-800-328-3895

Cover photograph © Pat O'Hara
Jacket design by Wayne C. Parmley
Book design and illustrations by Kenneth Hey

Printed and bound in U.S.A.

Library of Congress Cataloging-in-Publication Data

The healing earth : nature's medicine for the troubled soul / by Philip Sutton Chard.
  p. cm.
ISBN 1-55971-434-4
1. Nature--Psychological aspects. 2. Conducts of life. 3. Mental health I. Title
BF353.5.N37C45 1994
    155.9'1--dc20   94-21831
                                                        CIP

NATURE'S
MEDICINE
FOR THE
TROUBLED
SOUL

THE
HEALING
EARTH

CONTENTS

PREFACE

These days people seek knowledge, not wisdom.

Native American Healer Vernon Cooper

"**W**here do you suppose you came from?" my Godfather asked me.

For a 10-year-old that's a tough, embarrassing question, so I eyed him at first to make sure I wasn't being set up to play the pre-pubescent fool. But I need not have worried. Dennis Cavanaugh was a kind soul, and a bit of a mystic at that. At least as much a mystic as any Irish Catholic dairy farmer who made violins in his garage could expect to be, especially in the 1950s.

Given that, it seemed safe to answer.

"Well, from Mom . . . you know," I replied, blushing a bit.

"Yes, she bore you all right," he smiled, leaning in close to my face as he sometimes did at the chilling conclusion of one of his famous Saturday night ghost stories, those that sent my siblings and me scurrying for the sanctuary of denial under our bed covers.

"So that's where I came from," I echoed, sensing from the wry look behind his thick, rose-tinted glasses that I had answered only a small piece of a much larger question.

The warm wind whistled over our ears as he pointed to a dandelion jutting high above the squat grasses of my back yard.

"Where did that come from?" he pressed.

"A seed," I replied. "And the seed came from another plant . . . a mom dandelion, I guess."

"And the water?" he continued, pointing to the lake just a few yards away.

"Water isn't alive," I said, but his smile caused me to reconsider. "Is it?"

Mr. Cavanaugh was not one to hand over metaphysical answers on a cognitive platter. He knew that wisdom cannot be communicated straight away nor passed on like a family heirloom. It had to be experienced, felt, and fought for. He would point me in a direction, even give me a gentle shove, but the rest was my problem.

He was, as I sometimes tell my therapy clients in reference to myself, "a swimming instructor, not a lifeguard."

After a quarter century as a psychotherapist and emotional healer, I have learned to deeply appreciate and employ the wisdom of this simple, loving man. Staring into the eyes of countless souls wracked with emotional pain, blurred by drug abuse, overwhelmed by the demands of living, or confused by life's paradoxes and complexities, I have remembered Mr. Cavanaugh's art for sculpting personal transformation. By sheer example, he taught me to respect and nurture the innate healing capacities in each person, and to plant and cultivate the seeds of self-knowledge and change rather than try to force them to the surface.

"You just think about it," he suggested to me that afternoon, planting a seed within my intellect and soul. "Just think about where you really came from, about who your real mother is."

"But why?" I asked, perplexed.

"Because where you came from is your home, and when your heart hurts, as it will some day, you'll need to know how to get back home. That's where you get healed."

That was it, end of discussion. He left me sitting in the summer grass dumbfounded, with barely a clue, but with sufficient curiosity to fuel decades of wondering. And so I wondered—sometimes just out of curiousity, other times out of pain and confusion.

My Godfather's question walked and swam and slept with me, feeling the same earthen footfalls, the same waves and winds, watching the animals and plants and rocks, the clouds and storms and bright suns, smelling the pussy willows and trilliums and skunks, hearing the loons and the winter winds surfing the tops of pines. It listened to the teachers, preachers and scientists, read the books and journals, heard the opinions of countless geniuses and as many or more fools.

Until one day, decades past that steamy afternoon, it stopped being a question, as a few good questions are wont to do, and became an answer. Then I knew where I came from. I knew the face of my real Mother. I discovered how to be healed.

This book is about the answer.

A moment of your time, Mr. Cavanaugh, if you please.

I finally figured it out.

8

INTRODUCTION

Good books provoke us to think and to feel in gutsy, sensitive ways. However, often once we put a book down, the thoughts and feelings it catalyzed fade, like the remembrance of a vivid dream. Sure, we may recall how we were moved by a particular book for many years, or even be able to recite some of its most salient ideas, but often there are no visible signs in our person of what we have read.

Could someone tell by watching my behavior that I had read *The Bridges of Madison County* or *The Prophet* or *The Politics of Experience*? Probably not.

For a book to create discernible, sustaining change in someone's behavior it often requires more of a dialogue between author and reader. This is not a conversation in the traditional sense, but rather one in which the author suggests actions and the reader experiments accordingly. When a book convinces or stirs us to act in new ways, its impact on our lives may be permanent and ongoing—a living legacy of the power of words and concepts. Sometimes behavior change in response to a book's prodding is spontaneous—it just happens. In other instances, we must cultivate its suggested transformations, often by deliberately tinkering with new modes for conducting our lives.

It is my genuine hope that *The Healing Earth* will change not just your minds and hearts but also your behaviors. By transforming our actions, we transform our lives, and often the lives of others.

For those who find it useful to approach change in a premeditated fashion, at the conclusion of many of the book's chapters, I have included a "ceremony." These behavioral prescriptions offer ways to infuse your own life with new action, and so, new meaning. They present methods of personal renewal based upon profound contact with the healing capacities of the Earth. I encourage you to openly embrace these ceremonies, to discover through the conduits of your own senses whether the ideas in this book are more than mere concepts.

In addition to the ceremonies, some of the chapters speak for themselves in terms of behavior change and emotional healing. They present "how to" examples from my practice as a psychotherapist—experiences of others that may offer you ideas about creating healing ceremonies of your own. Also, the Epilogue contains a cornucopia of action-oriented approaches that may help sustain whatever heart-swell you experience from reading these pages.

Some of you may discover a "poor fit" between your nature and some of the book's ceremonies. If you work with them and end up feeling artificial or encumbered, this may represent a need to approach the Earth's healing powers along some other path. Hopefully, you will experience an intuitive sense of how to proceed. If nothing else, you may discover that simply spending time with our Mother, the Earth, may be healing in its own right.

I humbly hope this book changes your life.

Writing it has changed mine.

Philip Chard

UNNATURAL ORDER

Our lives are a cacophony; insulated from wind and rain and sun, from heat and cold, we are ensphered in our own catacombs of metal and concrete and plastic. Living in such a world, is it any wonder that we turn to drugs, to ever more sensational means of stimulation, to entertainment that renders us catatonic? Insulated from nature, ungrounded, why should we be surprised at our own brutality? Where, in such a world, is there room for gratitude, and for what should we be grateful?

Author Arthur Versluis

America is a society in decline. I'm not talking about the leading economic indicators, but rather about the emotional and spiritual health of individuals, families and communities. The signs of decay are everywhere—rampant child and elder abuse, rape, murder, gangs, drug and alcohol addiction, homelessness, environmental degradation, suicide, and what psychiatrists used to call "misery and unhappiness disorder." Call it what you will, the operative word is disorder. There are lots of theories to explain our downward spiral—the breakdown of families, the proliferation of drugs, demoralized schools, racism, economic lassitude, a crisis of moral values, sexism, and the other smoking guns so popular among politicians. But these are more symptoms than causes. *Why* are families disintegrating? What explains our penchant for self-destructive abuse of alcohol and other drugs? Why are children drawn to gangs and violence? Why do individuals feel alone, disconnected and unfulfilled?

Alienation tops my list of answers.

11

I don't mean alienation from society or the social order or "good old-fashioned values." I mean estrangement from the natural order, the most basic of orders, the one upon which all others—social, familial, psychological and spiritual—rest. The order of the Earth.

Each human being is a direct offspring of nature. And I mean *direct*. The air, water, land, and sun are as much our mothers and fathers as those people we call "mom and dad." You may think your biological parents gave you life but, fundamentally, they were simply conduits who transported your individual existence out from the unseen shadow of the life force and its mysterious energies and into the visible world of matter and form.

The Earth is our true Mother, our biological and existential home and our source and sustenance, but most of us are orphaned from her.

We spend much of our lives in artificial environments, immersed in metal, asphalt, glass, and plastic. Our daily interactions with things and happenings rarely involve trees, rivers, wind, soil, animals, clouds, or fields. Rather, we are busy interfacing with computers, charge cards, telephones, blow dryers, televisions, automobiles, pavement, bureaucracies, and each other. And we are emotionally destitute for it.

As many gardeners, naturalists, farmers, or outdoor types can tell you, a close relationship with natural things and processes grounds one's psyche and soul in the spiritual certainty of one's roots: the creation. Lose touch with nature's rhythms and you lose touch with your deepest self, with what the mystics call "the ground of your being."

Many of us have done just that. We run from the rain, curse the heat and cold, cower from storms and dark forests, abhor dirt, watch nature through TV screens and car windows, and prefer theaters, living rooms, or shopping malls to wooded glens, mountainsides, wetlands, and fields. Too few of us feel at home in our natural "house."

Cars, houses, offices—these artificial habitats are widely regarded as home, while the outdoors is perceived as "out there" and not *within* our own lives and consciousness. Our attitudes reflect this isolation.

In most people's thinking, food originates from a store, not from the miraculous alchemy of seed, sun, soil, and water. Adventure happens in a shopping mall or video game, not in a mysterious woods, on a windswept ridge, or afloat a choppy sea. Air is conditioned, heated, and treated, not inhaled in whole, fresh, billowing breaths. Weather is reported and watched through windows, not felt, except in furtive dashes from inside to inside, or on occasional vacations and sunny weekends.

Most folks identify more with sidewalks than woodland trails, more with boob tube graphics than blazing sunsets or the Milky Way, more with gas pedals than the feel of bare feet on grassy ground, more with 200 watt woofers than hoot owls or the wind whispering in the pines.

Try this experiment: lie on your stomach in the grass. How does this feel? Is it a foreign touch that greets your body, or the nurturing feel of life? Is it comforting to rest on the Earth's "skin," or do you feel weird, foolish, or out of place? Does the ground feel alive to you, or does it seem foreign, inert, and objectified?

Whatever you may or may not feel when you're in direct contact with the Earth, she is our Mother, and we are all babes suckling at her breast.

Just a flowery metaphor? No. More like rock-hard reality.

A farm field, a lake, the air, trees, bees, clouds—they may not seem to directly sustain your existence, but they do. Yet often when ecologists proclaim our utter dependence on the life force that permeates the Earth, people react with puzzlement, ho-hum, or outright scorn. This distance that alienates so many from the Earth now threatens our very survival as a species. It has already wreaked havoc with our spiritual well-being as individuals and as a culture.

In an evolutionary sense, our species is like a newborn that cannot survive for long without its mother, yet many of us seem hell-bent upon matricide.

Many of us understand this intellectually, but few of us believe it in our bones.

And the analogy does not end with bio-systems. The absence of emotional bonding between humans and their Earth Mother is a psychological and spiritual crisis as well as an ecological one. Not only do we abuse the biological supports that nature has created to sustain all creatures, but among us there is a growing disdain for all life: for other creatures, fellow members of our species, and even our own individual lives. Survival is often a function of relationships, of parent to offspring, of individual to tribe, of species to habitat. This is true of emotional, as well as physical, survival.

Our psychological and spiritual subsistence as individuals, and that of our society as a whole, is intensely dependent upon a heartfelt bond between us and our Earth Mother. All the critical variables that psychology pinpoints as cornerstones for good mental health—a sense of belonging and community, self-worth, purpose, faith, hope, gratitude, and a connection with the sacred—begin with the relationship between each person and the Earth. The symptoms of our alienation from nature are evident:

- Many of us feel emotionally and spiritually estranged from the natural environment. Nature seems foreign and foreboding. It has the feel of "not me."
- Our academic community is obsessed with studying and labeling nature, with scientifically dissecting its individual elements and processes, but most of us spend little time *experiencing* it. We hold nature at an intellectual arm's length. As Sam Keen, author and modern philosopher, has asked, what might a science be like that was created by men who loved their mothers? Or by people who loved their Mother Earth?
- For most, our relationship with nature is based on the desire to exert control, to bend the natural world to our will and wishes. We feel little gratitude or respect. Like the spoiled, thoughtless child, we take our Mother for granted and expect her to selflessly comply with our every whim and demand.

- In our hearts, most of us perceive the Earth as an "it," not as a "thou." We have deluded ourselves into believing that nature is a thing rather than a living entity.

These delusions have deadened us. Without the succor of our Earth Mother, the life-sustaining force that we commonly call "the will to live" mutates into an equally powerful death wish. If we ignore or sever the emotional and spiritual umbilical cord that binds us with the Earth, then its living vitality will no longer nurture us, and like any child deprived of touch, loving, and tenderness, we will die a psychological death—what the French call "the little death." When the little death leaves one's psyche and spirit cold and lifeless, then the unconscious desire for obliteration (the death wish) fills the vacuum. Produce enough individuals with a death wish and you get a society with a collective death wish.

Perhaps this is what we have.

Am I trying to dump all our social and individual ills at the doorstep of paradise lost? No. There have always been violence, hate, poverty, and madness, even in cultures that were rooted in a balanced relationship with the natural world. It is easy to romanticize nature and the "noble savage," but as modern human animals, we cannot live and act like our brethren creatures or native ancestors. We have evolved to the point where we don't have to eat each other to survive, where we can adapt (albeit artificially) to many diverse and arduous habitats, and where we can glorify the creation in art and music. Unfortunately, these accomplishments have convinced us that we stand apart from the rest of nature, and have lead us to confront our modern social and individual problems by relying on technology, politics, law enforcement, and psychology, rather than the guidance and healing inherent in the natural world. But without this natural sustenance, we just aren't up to the task of emotional and spiritual healing that looms before us.

Without her, we will fail.

We forget that there is more wisdom in the voices of wind and water than can be found in any talk show, self-help tome, or politician; that there is as much spiritual sustenance in a night sky or a misty morning as an ornate cathedral or charismatic sermon; and that there is more life-purpose in growing a garden than in many careers, and more education in exploring a marsh, pond, or prairie than can be gained from months in a classroom.

If each of us spent more time with our hands in the dirt, our faces in the wind, our eyes on the wonderment of creation, and our bodies cradled in the arms of Mother Earth, I suspect there'd be far less affliction in this world and in our hearts.

If we are to go forward, both as individuals and as a culture, we must first go back.

Back to the Earth.

NATURE AS HEALER

*I am not . . . addressing myself to the happy possessors
of faith, but to those many people for whom the light has
gone out, the mystery has faded, and God is dead.*

Psychoanalyst C. C. Jung

Psychotherapy is popular these days, made
more so by the growing number of people
who feel emotionally and spiritually lost.
That constitutes a lot of us. At one time or
another, probably all of us belong to these
unhappy ranks.

"Their misery is my prosperity," a mis-
guided colleague once remarked in reference to how many folks seem to be looking
for "the answers" on the ceiling above the
shrink's couch, and shelling out big bucks in
the process. There is an unhappy truth buried in his cynicism.

While many critics cite our widespread consumption of counseling,
psychoanalysis, self-help books, support groups, and New Age theology
as evidence that we have become a society of whiners, entitlement-
laden brats, and self-absorbed neurotics, it's also possible that we are
a nation of lost souls. Lost people go looking. We line up behind pop
psychology gurus, televangelists, and other self-appointed experts
because they promise us clarity and peace—the answers. Their list of
promised answers is long, but their list of actual ones is fairly short.

While it is an oversimplification, most of the people who come to me for psychotherapy (best described as "talk therapy") have a lost look in their eyes. Not just the look of someone who is confused or vexed about one particular life problem like a troubled marriage, an addiction, or stressful job, but the look of someone who can't find the way home. "The lost puppy look" is how a woman colleague describes it.

Most of us have wandered away from our emotional and spiritual home in the Earth, and we can't find a way back. So, like the city slicker lost in the forest, we stumble about in a mild panic (the proverbial "quiet desperation"), circling endlessly, searching for someone who can show us "the way." As Richard Alpert, a psychologist-turned-sage, so aptly described it:

" . . . people were constantly looking into my eyes, like 'Do you know?' Just that subtle little look, and I was constantly looking into their eyes - 'Do you know?' And there we were . . . and there was always that feeling that everybody was very close and we all knew we knew, but nobody quite knew."

It took me 15 years or so of practicing psychotherapy to figure out that I didn't have what my clients were looking for, that I didn't possess the answers they sought, and that nobody else did either. All of us were looking for "home" in the deepest psychological and spiritual sense of that term. In our souls and hearts all of us retain a faint but compelling memory of our spiritual connection with the Earth, like the background energy permeating the cosmos left over from the big bang, but after many years of being too civilized, few can lock onto the signal.

While I believe that psychotherapy can be helpful in addressing emotional and spiritual issues, talk alone does not assist people in regaining their sense of home. Talk therapy may help someone shore up a sagging marriage, throttle back on a light-speed lifestyle, or become a more disciplined parent, but it doesn't restore a heartfelt sense of belonging and meaning. It doesn't return us to our wellspring in the life force. It doesn't heal the wound of separation from our natural world.

Psychotherapy may teach people how to walk, so to speak, but not which direction to walk. It provides methods, not answers.

Like most psychotherapists, I discovered this by observing my clients. Honest shrinks will admit they learn more from their clients than their clients do from them. Over time, my clients taught me that talk, behavior change, catharsis, insight development, and all the other tricks of my trade go only so far, and that's not far enough for many. Without question one's life is better when, for instance, the drinking stops, the relationships heal, the pace of living becomes humane, and people become better communicators, but improvements in behavior do not heal the deep wounds of the psyche and soul. We may become better at being lost, yet remain lost just the same.

It is when we know who we are, why we are, and where we belong, that the ever-present problems of living become easier to bear, and make more sense. But when one is confused about the who, why, and where of one's existence, life's daily difficulties feel like sheer, ice-covered cliffs placed before us by arbitrary and cruel fate.

To help my clients be less lost and more healed, I began to experiment with reacquainting them with our Earth Mother. When they would give me that "Do you know?" look, I would more or less respond with, "No, but I know who does." When I would tell them, in so many words, that the one who knows is the Earth, many initially found this notion, to paraphrase them, "simplistic." A lot of folks wouldn't embrace the concept that our planet is wise, giving, and sacred. Too many couldn't escape thinking of the Earth as a dumb rock with some water and greenery on top, so it was tough convincing many of them to give this sort of "treatment" a fair try.

But a few did. They had the courage and faith to return to our Earth as a source of emotional healing, as a way to go from being lost to being found. It was through their experiences that I grew to understand the latent power of the Earth as an agent of healing. And while I had high expectations for this approach, even I was surprised by the capacity of the Earth to restore balance to our emotional lives.

The remainder of this book is about this wondrous healing process, one which has become the mainstay of my practice as a psychotherapist, and which has profoundly influenced my own existence. What I share with you is not original. I did not invent this stuff. Our intuitive knowledge of the Earth's healing power has been evident in our species for millennia.

I hope to place this understanding within our modern context. In this regard, I have much yet to learn. But what I have learned, I will share with you. I am thankful for your interest, and I hope these ideas serve you well.

ORPHANS FROM LIFE

It's a different kind of world to grow up in when you're out in the forest with the little chipmunks and the great owls. All these things are around you as presences, representing forces and powers and magical possibilities of life that are not yours and yet are all part of life, and that opens it out to you. Then you find it echoing in yourself, because you are nature.

Anthropologist Joseph Campbell

If you've ever watched a baby interact with her or his mother for the first time, and then observed that same child during initial contact with the natural world, then it's likely you have seen the same wide-eyed countenance twice.

Wonder. Awe. Absorption. Attachment.

In our youngest times, we do not distinguish between human mother and Earth Mother. We recognize both instinctively. One is the conduit of the life force, the other its source, and both bear the face of belonging, of home.

We come out of our mothers, both of them, knowing deep in our emotional sinew who they are, because we are of them and through them. This is not a mental construct or a philosophical position. We experience it in our bones, our cells, and synapses, because we are made of the stuff of life. All our parts, including our brains and consciousness, are crafted from the raw materials of the Earth.

As Joni Mitchell sings, "We are star dust, and we got to get ourselves back to the garden. . ."

Indeed. Earth is star dust that coalesced into a rocky ball and then came alive. And each of us is part of that coming alive, of animate matter emerging miraculously out of inert stuff. We are participants in this living experiment. The ever-pregnant Earth keeps squeezing out new organic possibilities made of its own self—carbon, water, and hydrogen in myriad permutations. Again, as Joseph Campbell, the renowned anthropologist, so aptly described it:

"I once saw a marvelous scientific movie about protoplasm. It was a revelation to me. It is in movement all the time, flowing. Sometimes it seems to be flowing this way and that, and then it shapes things. It has a potentiality for bringing things into shape. I saw this movie in northern California, and as I drove down the coast to Big Sur, all the way, all I could see was protoplasm in the form of grass being eaten by protoplasm in the form of cows; protoplasm in the form of birds diving for protoplasm in the form of fish. You just got this wonderful sense of the abyss from which all has come. But each form has its own intentions, its own possibilities . . ."

By any reasonable analysis, this process is a miracle. That few of us appreciate the miraculous quality of our own existence and that of our living brethren and our home planet, is testimony to how far we have wandered from knowing who we are.

About knowing who we are: We can call ourselves whatever we want—human, person, individual, "me" or by our many legal and social names—but at the most basic of levels, each of us is a child of the Earth. We are no more separate from the whole of the Earth than is a bubble from the atmosphere of air in which it floats. Only the slimmest of films (our skin) convinces us to believe in our separateness from the rest of life's teeming sea. Nonetheless, many of us blindly accept the illusion of being separate.

The obvious reality of our origin in the Earth escapes the finely tuned intellects of most adults. It is a felt-knowledge, rather than a cognitive one. In contrast, many children intuitively know this truth that adults have forgotten—at least until we convince them otherwise, which occurs very early for most.

Usually, this "you are separate" brainwashing begins by keeping a baby largely detached from his or her Earth Mother. Little ones are immersed in cribs, cars, bedrooms, and boob tubes, but rarely in grass, soil, clouds, trees, wind, rain, snow, and all the other touches of the natural world. Many children grow up all but cut off from nature, the same way most adults live. They are sequestered in artificial, controlled environments that remove them from the feel of the life force. We create bubbles inside of bubbles inside of bubbles—more layers and boundaries to keep the "outside" out. Most of our children live as bubble babies, and grow up to be prisoners of technology and materialism.

It is not uncommon for a child to be rushed from car to house, to car to school, to car to doctor's office, experiencing only fleeting episodes of outside. By way of analogy, this would be like showing a baby only transient glimpses of her or his mother. Eventually, mom would become a cameo player in the passing images of life, like some disembodied portrait of a once-present, now-absent ancestor. That is how the Earth Mother is to most of us—unreal, ephemeral, abstract. Gone.

Given the chance, most of us would not grow up this way. The call of our Earth Mother is strong within our hearts, even at an early age.

When I was about six years into this life, a blizzard bore down upon our lakeside home in northern Illinois. My father was out delivering fuel oil to his rural customers, and my mother and four older siblings were scattered in the many nooks and crannies of our two-story, Victorian home, content to occupy themselves with inside pursuits. But I was riveted to the bay window in our living room. I couldn't have explained it in these words at the time, but I was swooning in awe of our Earth Mother.

My eyes beheld the splendor of our oh-so-common side yard; a large, glen-like rectangle bordered on one end by several century-old black walnut trees and at the other by a solitary, elderly elm. A blur of blinding white powdery air poured into the open fold created by these aged trees. My rapture at this beatific sight was interrupted by my mother's entrance.

"It's really coming down," she remarked on her way to the parlor.

"Mom, I wanna go out," I requested.

She stopped in mid-stride.

"Out there? In the blizzard? It's storming too hard," she concluded.

"Please, Mom. I'll dress good," I pressed. Everything about me, except my body itself, was already outside that window.

The understanding smile that rippled across her face told me the case was won. After arduous preparations, I emerged from the front door of our house like an astronaut from an air lock, layered and buffered from the frigid elements. As I lumbered, robot-like, toward the side yard, the faces of the house's inhabitants appeared in the bay window, observing my progress and cracking jokes. But no matter, for I was within the mystery. I was exploring where I had come from. My roots. Our roots.

The wind howled with its limitless power, spinning my body in a vortex of heavy whiteness. It seemed I was swimming in a miraculous ether, submerged in the primordial soup that adults were always trying to get me to climb out of. With a plop I sat in the rising snow and squinted up into the formless sky, straining to see in that whiteness the source of all the magnificence around me and to comprehend the rapture within my heart. And in a manner of seeing that is not the province of our eyes or minds, I perceived what was invisible within the storm. I "saw" the implicit mover that was creating the explicit movement, the invisible wind that moves the tree, the unseen energy that makes the wave, the power that lifts the shoot from the seed, the spirit that the ancients knew as Mother Earth. I beheld this whatever-it-is that is the maker of happenings, beheld it as one would the faint glow of a still distant dawn or an almost departed sunset.

And I knew in the marrow of my soul the look of our Mother. And that is the source of the most elemental and certain joy. Toys and trinkets, theme parks and video games, hot clothes and movies, money and success can bring fun or adventure or a sense of being cool, but deep-seated and unshakable joy comes from perceiving one's bond with the life force. It is the joy of knowing "I belong."

This sort of happening is not so profound and unusual that only a few can experience it. Time with the Earth Mother is mystical, but incense-burning and mantra-chanting are not necessary. My brief communion in the blizzard was an ordinary moment in an ordinary child's life, made sacred by a way of seeing, a way of being; not by what was done, owned, said or achieved, but by what was experienced. These times are available to all of us.

From early on, we are visited by such moments, by these reminders of our heritage in the Earth. As children no one need teach us how to recognize our Mother, but to retain this sense we often require affirmation and support from our family and social community, which is rarely forthcoming these days. Instead, as children we are sent very explicit messages about who mother really is. Mother is that human female who teaches you to call her "mom." Any references to "the Earth Mother" are couched in analogy and metaphor, and are not to be taken literally, but rather as figures of speech intended to illustrate (in an intellectual sense) our dependence upon the Earth for food, water, and oxygen.

A few adults have retained this remembrance of Earth-as-Mother, and so seek to convey it to their own children. Traditional Native American spirituality has served as a caretaker of this intrinsic knowledge. Members of the Iroquois Nation, for example, teach their offspring that all people come from the Earth. They speak of unborn generations of children "whose faces are coming from beneath the ground." For them, Earth-as-Mother is more than a compelling idea. They feel it in their hearts.

In contrast, by the time most of us are adults, we have lost this comprehension of our origins in nature. To most, the Earth is a rock that we drive and jet around on, play tennis and golf across, mow, excavate, landfill, plunder for raw materials and groceries, and get buried in. We do not feel the Earth as the living, ever-changing goddess that bore us from her fertile womb. She is a thing to be used, to be looked at through car windows, and to be experienced skin-to-elements only on the best of days.

The absence of the felt knowledge that Earth is our Mother causes great suffering, both for individuals and for our society. Without it, we are fundamentally lost, confused, and spiritually misshapen. When our carefully crafted social or emotional security systems crumble under the onslaught of a divorce, victimization, financial failure, or the death of a loved one, there is no ground upon which to stand. We feel the cold void where the nexus with the Earth Mother should be.

Most of us have become motherless children.

We are orphans from life.

STRANGERS IN OUR OWN LAND

Why do people run from the rain,
like they run from trouble and pain?
It's only there to help you,
there's no need to be afraid . . .

The Sons of Champlin

Ellen ran from the rain and wind, the cold, snow, and heat. She cowered from all but the finest of sunny days. And that common behavior said a great deal about her as a person. It says much about many of us.

The October afternoon when she first came to my psychotherapy office, I glimpsed her crossing the street from my second story window. It's my custom to try to picture new clients, sight unseen, on the basis of our initial telephone conversation, and then pick them out from the crowd. I felt certain it was she I saw dashing through the day's drizzle, brought by a chilly wind from Lake Michigan, a few blocks east of my digs.

Ellen had that customary, civilized look about her as she scurried for the sanctuary behind the building door. Her eyes squinted as she tugged her rain coat up over her left shoulder, hoping to block out the moisture and cold, and an expression of pain and worry wrinkled her countenance. She appeared under attack, like a soldier scurrying from sniper fire. But "the enemy" was not poised on some rooftop with a high-powered rifle. For her, it was swirling in the moist wind.

Watching her, my mind flashed on the image of Dean Shipman, the scruffy old salt who taught me to sail the Great Lakes. Never one to let a storm interfere with making way, Dean always held course in a blow, even a full gale. On one such occasion, I looked up from my corner of his sailboat's cockpit, where I clung for dear life against the howling wind and breaking seas to see him face forward into a driving spindrift that spit like nails. He was soaked and spattered, but smiling. He didn't flinch from the storm, but met it full open, like an animal in his element. "Like a pig in slop," as he was fond of saying.

Just after some wash from a wave breaking on the bow had blasted him a good one, he looked down at me with an honest, gleeful smile, sputtering water from his mouth.

"Isn't this great!" he bellowed over the wind's howl in the rigging.

For him, the natural world is not an enemy.

Ellen interrupted my nautical nostalgia when she burst through the office door, harried and hurried.

"I'm sorry for being late. Are you Philip Chard?"

"Yup, that's what they call me," I replied, extending my hand.

"Boy, this weather is really terrible." She made conversation and also made a statement about her alienation from the Earth, and from her own deeper self that, in all of us, is a reflection of the natural world.

"I find this weather mysterious," I replied. She looked puzzled.

"Mysterious?"

"Yes, the mist drifting in the wind and that fog beginning to roll in off the lake carry a tone of mystery," I explained. "For me."

"You like being cold and wet?" she asked, wondering about her choice of therapists.

"I appreciate being cold and wet. Storms aren't always enjoyable or comfortable, but I do appreciate them, and I learn from them," I replied.

"Learn?" She looked blatantly confused.

"Yes. We can learn from adversity when we don't hide from it, so I don't avoid storms. But you do."

"Yes, I do." She looked puzzled once again. "Shouldn't I?"

"Could I venture a presumptuous guess about you, Ellen?" I asked.

"Well, sure, go ahead." She granted permission, despite our having just met.

"You avoid a lot of uncomfortable things in your life, and I don't just mean the weather," I guessed. "You're running away a lot these days."

Her tears confirmed my hunch. Like many of us, Ellen ran not only from the rain, but also from her emotional storms, like her anger, sadness, and fear. Just as we turn away and hide from the Earth's harsher moods, so many of us flee our emotional discomforts until, like Ellen, we have no place left to hide. How we feel about the Earth, is often a reflection of how we feel toward our inner being, which we derive from the Earth.

I don't routinely diagnose people by how they behave in adverse weather conditions, but I often do evaluate the degree of attachment or detachment a person feels in relation to the Earth Mother. Alienation from the Earth and alienation from one's self often go hand-in-hand. Folks who avoid nature have often made a lifestyle of evading their own *inner* nature as well, which has storms all its own.

Many folks, like Ellen, perceive the Earth as an adversary, a nuisance and a persecutor, except on those unusual occasions when sky conditions, humidity, temperature, and wind are within a narrowly ideal range and there are no bugs. Given the power, most of us would regulate the Earth's atmosphere with the same thermostatic aplomb we apply to home heating and cooling, and we would apply the same obsessive control to our emotional lives, as well.

Why do people run from the rain?

For the same reason that children run from strangers. For the same reason adults run from depression, conflict, and fear. They feel disaffected from what is euphemistically called "the elements," and so perceive danger in that which feels foreign, that which has the feel of "not me." Ellen is repelled by what a naturalist friend of mine calls "Mother Nature's French kiss"—the moist feel of rain on the face.

For most of us, the Earth is a stranger, and we fear her, or at least regard her with wariness. In turn, we fear our own inner nature—that which we derived from the Earth.

This widespread alienation from the touch of our natural world is a defining aspect of modern American society. Most of us have made a lifestyle of avoiding wind, snow, heat, cold, rain, dirt, hard ground, choppy water, outdoor darkness, and tough terrain. We seek to evade almost anything we can't control, anything we don't find in our living rooms or automobiles. And when we make a habit of sidestepping nature, often we also end up shunning the inner self that is a reflection of the natural world.

We don't begin life this way. As children, most of us delight in mixing it up with the Earth's many physical manifestations, and we seek her ministrations with the same attraction as a baby suckling its mother's breast.

As a five-year-old, I made a habit of jumping into a large mud puddle that appeared in our backyard baseball field right around home plate after each heavy rain. To get the most pronounced SPLAT! from my landings, I sometimes hauled out my Radio Flyer wagon for use as a diving platform.

Upon returning home after one of these gritty immersions, my human mother greeted me at the kitchen door, while a visiting friend looked on, aghast.

"Well, you really got into it this time," Mom said, giggling while trying to act cross but doing an unconvincing job.

"Why . . . he's absolutely filthy!" the friend erupted.

"Take it easy, Helen," my mom replied. "It's only dirt, and pretty good dirt at that."

Before we brainwash children with the mistaken notion that they are not offspring of the Earth, they revel in the natural world, undaunted by rain, snow, mud, grass stains, wind and cold lakes; all the experiences their parents seek to protect them from. Before long, many of them learn from the adults in their midst that getting wet, dirty, ruffled, sweaty, or otherwise imprinted by the Earth is to be discouraged and, if necessary, corrected. As many put it, "After all, you aren't an animal."

How untrue.

I've fallen into this Earth-as-nuisance frame of mind on occasion. On one of my frequent excursions to the high plains of North America, I happened upon an elderly Lakota man outside a convenience store not far from the Black Hills.

"Boy, it's mighty hot," I said to him, wiping sweat from my brow and squinting up at the blazing sun.

He nodded in tolerant recognition of my complaint, peered up at the sizzling sky and then looked my way with a little grin.

"The sun likes us today. It wants to be close," he replied, and then strolled away.

Ellen, like most of us, like myself that day on the plains, experiences her Earth Mother as an aggravation, an opponent, or even a tormentor. Like a spoiled, unappreciative child, she has no gratitude for the forces that created and sustain her. Consequently, she also experiences her own nature as an aggravation, an opponent and, at times, a tormentor. She has no gratitude for the "unpleasant" emotional forces working within her. Our attitude toward our Earth Mother frequently mirrors our posture toward our inner self.

Like so many of us today, Ellen has no bond with the Earth. She feels lost, alienated, and alone, and while she may attribute her disquiet to stress, conflicted relationships, and low self-esteem, the genesis of her disquiet resides in being alienated from her source, from the Earth and, so, from her own innermost self. No multitude of friends, therapists or obsessive pursuits can give her what she needs.

She needs to feel at home.

At home with the Earth.

GOING HOME

Lose your mind, and come to your senses.

Psychoanalyst Fritz Perls

I took Noreen to a state park for our psychotherapy session.

Like many parks, this one was set-aside land once deemed of little economic value with topography that imposed too many obstacles to be monopolized for profit. The landscape boasted high limestone cliffs, forming an escarpment several hundred feet above the fast-running river that bisected the terrain. All of it except for a few patches of prairie was covered by old oak, elm, and maple.

It was Noreen's third session of psychotherapy, but the first outside my office.

"Why are we here?" she asked as I spread a blanket on some open ground in an oak glen.

"To listen," I replied, deliberately vague.

"Seems kind of weird," she grumbled, sitting on the blanket, scanning for bugs and squinting from the press of the uneven ground beneath her.

I smiled to myself but made no effort to dissuade her sour, I'm-not-getting-into-this attitude. Noreen's perspective was typical, through no fault of her own. For her, being in the oak glen was weird, while being in a noisy, thing-strewn, stale-air office was normal.

Noreen had come to me with vague but bothersome symptoms, as we euphemistically call messages from the inner self to its less cognizant outer cousin, the so-called conscious mind. Hers included obsessive worrying, a nagging sense of apprehension (about what, she couldn't say), and persistent fears of "being alone and on my own." Nothing mind-shattering, but sufficient angst to render her life quite unpleasant. When she asked me to paste a diagnostic label on her, I opted for "homesickness." You won't find that one in the Diagnostic and Statistical Manual of mental disorders, but you should be able to. It's plenty prevalent.

"Please close your eyes and listen," I asked Noreen once she had settled on the blanket. She was kind enough to comply.

There were no other humans nearby on that weekday in June. The sun still held high in the late afternoon, and there was an uncertain wind. By any city or suburban standard, it was wonderfully quiet. As happens when one nestles down in the outdoors and blends with the natural surroundings, our Earth Mother soon began to show herself. First came a squirrel bounding through the dry grass, trekking from one tree to the next.

"What's that?" Noreen asked, a tad alarmed.

"A sound," I said.

"I know it's a sound! What's making it?"

"Just listen to the sound," I suggested. She frowned but still complied.

Soon the squirrel's crunchy footfalls transformed into scampering scratchings as it ascended the oak. Noreen's head tilted to catch more of this new resonance. Then she was pulled away by the call of a cardinal, its shrill and pedantic voice searching the woods for its mate, which soon replied.

"What kind of bird is that?" Noreen asked, then corrected herself. "Never mind. Just listen."

And so it went for our 50-minute hour. The Earth spoke and Noreen listened. After awhile, Noreen lay back on the blanket, letting one hand stroke the grass while the other rested across her heart. She stopped trying to label everything and let the sounds wash over her—the birds and chipmunks, the hovering dragonflies, the squirrels vaulting from branch to branch, the river's rush in the background, and the occasional rustle of cottonwood leaves in the come-and-go breeze.

Gradually, the hard lines on her forehead relaxed. Her breathing slowed and deepened. Occasionally, a smile rippled across her countenance, as if she were remembering something pleasant from long ago. All signs of worry, apprehension, and fears for her future drifted off her face.

When we drove off in my car, she stepped back into her thinking mind.

"What was that for?" she asked, still peaceful. "Just to get me to relax?"

"You told me that when you were a child, your mother used to read you stories and sing you lullabies," I recounted.

"Yes, that's true."

"And what did that do for you?"

"It made me feel close to her, and safe."

"Well, your other Mother just sang you some lullabies. How did that feel?" I inquired.

Noreen puzzled on my words a few moments before she spoke.

"It *is* the same feeling," she said more to herself than to me, a tad amazed.

Then a tear or two trickled across her sad but hopeful smile.

Noreen quickly developed the habit of visiting her Mother whenever her soul needed soothing. While she is particularly fond of the Earth's lullabies, she has indulged her other senses, as well—seeing, touching, and smelling. And she always comes back from these visits feeling like a child who knows she has a home, no matter what.

And she does have a home.

We all do.

As we are so often told, home is a place of the heart. We know home not by an address, but through a feeling of attachment, of "this is my place and I belong here." Home is not some stationary edifice, but rather any place that offers safe harbor for the human heart and spiritual sustenance for the soul. When we are beset by emotional storms, we seek it. And while home can be found among our families and friends (at least for the fortunate among us), the emotional "place" made by our fellow humans can be uncertain and capricious.

Many of us have gone home to loved ones in times of emotional need, only to feel ignored, hurried along or, worse yet, cast out. Granted, some of us are so blessed that we can always rely on someone to be our "home," but many cannot. Often, human acceptance is highly conditional.

Yet we all have another home with our Earth Mother, and though our species has done her grievous harm over the last century, she still takes us in when we come calling. Once we begin to feel at home in the woods and waters, mountains, deserts, prairies, and skies, then we always have a sanctuary. We can invariably go home to the lullabies of her sounds, the "stories" of her daily dramas, the touches of her winds and weathers, and the familiar rhythms of her cycles.

When my psychotherapy clients are feeling emotionally homeless, which is often, I take them back to that abode which, deep in their spirits, they remember as the domicile of their Earth Mother, their heart's first home. I encourage them to revisit the myriad sensations that remind them of that greater family—the conclave of nature—of which we all are a part.

And most do remember.

This is not surprising. This remembering is latent in our biological substance, in the very matter that constitutes us and all else in nature. It is the most elemental of memories. Body memory. Genetic memory. Soul memory. The kind that recalls our bond with the Earth through the very feeling of being flesh and blood.

So we simply remember who we are. Not in an intellectual sense. Not like the philosopher pondering "Who am I?" or "To be or not to be," but as a feeling, sensing creature that revisits its source. In some fashion, we become like the salmon or the giant sea turtles returning to their birthplaces to spawn and lay eggs, or like the whales, geese and caribou in their great migrations. Remembering the way, the place, the home.

Once we have forgotten the way home and lost the bond with the Earth, we begin to encounter the experience of alienation, of being strange, disconnected, and without a place in life. We become homeless in the most profound and existential sense of that term, like some creature that awakens from a sleep not remembering the who, why, where, or when of its existence.

Fortunately, the way home is not so difficult to find again. A small park, the shade of a nearby tree, a creek or lakeshore, a backyard garden, all can suffice just as well, and more conveniently than an alpine peak, a wilderness trail, or a wave-swept sea. When we visit our Earth Mother, even in her small places, to listen, watch, and feel, then we remember. There, our hearts can find all that any heart needs: acceptance, love, mystery, belonging, wonder, and hope.

Certainly, it is not always so simple as sitting in the woods, walking the beach, climbing a hilltop, or meandering in an open field. Turning off one's cognitive shredder is difficult. The thinking mind can drown out our awareness of the sensations that nature uses to call us home, and we can't always leave our worries and troubles behind when we depart the office or the house and strike out for wilder places.

But it is the place to start, even for those of us who are long estranged from our source in nature. Like the prodigal son or daughter, we must first make the journey home, and then petition to enter. This petitioning is accomplished by making the mental effort to be in the here and now, the present place and time, while in our Mother's domicile. This can be as simple as meditating upon a natural object for a few minutes, such as a leaf, stone, feather, acorn, flower, or icicle. Or one can focus on a particular mode of sensory contact by listening to wind or water, smelling plants and flowers, tasting wild berries and fruits (please determine what you're tasting first), touching any of the Earth's myriad textures, or visually absorbing her wondrous colorations.

One must lose the mind and come back to the senses, back to the language of the Earth. Again, it's easier said than satisfied, especially for those of us who make our livings by thinking, planning, and worrying, but it can be done.

Just visit home. Nature is still there. It will call you in. All you need do is listen, smell, taste, see, and touch. Thinking is unnecessary and distracting.

After all, you are not a thought.

You are a creature.

You are a child of the Earth.

EXERCISE:

CEREMONY OF RE-BONDING

A simple way to "go home" and renew the bond with our Earth Mother is through sensory immersion in the wind. This ceremony can be done anywhere outdoors and in virtually any setting - your back yard, in front of your office building, a park, in a convertible, or walking down the street.

- Pause from your thinking and business of everyday life.
- Bring your awareness to the feel of the Earth's breath (the wind) moving around your skin and body. The atmosphere is always moving, even if this motion is barely perceptible.
- Notice how our Mother's breath is touching you. Depending upon the strength and consistency of the wind, its touch may feel gentle, firm, playful, or rough.
- If you feel comfortable doing so in your setting, turn your face to the direction of the the wind, open your arms wide, and embrace it in return.
- Finally, breathe in the air deeply and then whisper (or shout) your thanks. It is our Mother's breath that makes possible our own life-sustaining respirations.

SIX

DEADNESS

The old Lakota was wise. He knew that man's heart away from nature becomes hard; he knew that lack of respect for growing, living things soon led to lack of respect for humans too.

Lakota Chief Luther Standing Bear

There is a tree outside my mother's home in Delavan, Wisconsin, that is a creature of majesty and grace, deserving the awe and homage of any Homo Sapiens fortunate enough to wander beneath its branches.

But it receives no reverence.

This very old silver maple measures 16 feet around at its base. About ten feet above its tenacious grip on the ground, the trunk explodes into half a dozen main branches that ascend 150 feet or more, splaying out in myriad tributaries that together compose a sheltering arc that shades a broad expanse of the Earth. In its stately realm reside birds and squirrels, butterflies, beetles, chipmunks, and insects galore. Hundreds of children have cavorted among its stout branches for many generations, leaving occasional signs of their passing. It has held ropes for swings, suffered the carving of lover's hearts, bent before thousands of storms, slept through its many winters and burst anew each spring, and watched the passing of whole human lives.

Yet hardly a soul pays it heed.

A few may curse its wondrous showers of pastel leaves in the autumn or the "helicopter" seeds it garnishes upon the Earth each spring, but they usually regard this grand, living being with all the consideration one would afford a cord of fire wood. Maybe less.

We are reaching that unhappy place in our cultural history where even the living creatures around us appear lifeless, inert, and objectified. Animals are to hunt, to eat, to stare at through a zoo's Plexiglas, or to dislodge from their dens or nests because they leave marks on our golf-green lawns and manicured gardens. To most, trees are paper, cardboard, or joists awaiting the harvest, or decorations for our landscapes, or hindrances to the next bypass, sidewalk, or dream house. A lake or river is "just a lot of water," as a particularly jaded fellow once told me. The atmosphere exists to make us happy when it is warm and sunny, or to tick us off when it isn't.

Our siblings in life, these other children of our common Mother, now appear dead to most of us. We perceive them as things, much as we view cars, CD players, or easy chairs. In fact, some people hold far more affection for their automobiles than for the trees and rabbits in their backyards or the birds singing outside their windows each morning.

But our jaded vision works both ways.

When our eyes stop seeing and our hearts cease valuing the other life forms and processes that the Earth has created, they also cease to perceive and honor human life.

"Nobody respects the value of human life anymore," many folks lament.

An overstatement, to be sure, but it seems more true all the time. The circle comes around. As our hearts grow dead to the life forms surrounding us, they deaden to our own life form, as well. We become like the brother or sister who has rejected siblings and family. Our cold rebuff and hatred of our kin turns inward, eating through to our own hearts. The creatures, elements, and processes of the Earth are our kin, as well.

More and more, our indifference and antipathy toward life is becoming hatred of our own life form. As one looks around at our society, this self-hatred is sadly evident. Psychologically and socially, we are ripping ourselves asunder.

"It is matricide," a pained environmentalist told me in reference to our species' proclivity for ecological carnage. "We are killing our Mother."

It is the sin of sins to turn with death in your soul toward that which put life in your heart and body. And our matricide is rapidly becoming suicide.

This killing is far more subtle than dumping toxic wastes in the watershed, torching a rain forest, or driving animals to extinction. It is a killing that comes from our minds, not just our landfills, tailpipes, factories, and air conditioners. Once we have looked upon the Earth with the cold eyes of deadness, once we have passed over to the kind of seeing that takes what is alive and, through jaded consciousness, transforms it into an inert piece of matter, a raw material for economic exploitation, then the transition is complete. We begin to experience *ourselves* as things, as dead, as stuff to be used up but not valued.

Alienation becomes absolute. The absence of a bond with the Earth begins to erode our interpersonal connections with each other, and it wears away the internal emotional bonds that integrate each individual into a whole person. Not only do we become estranged from the living world, from our source in Nature and from each other, but also from our own souls, for we are part of the living world—or part of the dead world if that is how we see it.

In such a state of spirit, there is no such thing as "mental health" or "a good family life" or "a kinder, gentler society." There is only the blank stare of eyes that no longer see the living sun, or a billowing cloud carried across the sky by the wind, or the endless shades of color in a sunset. Behind such a stare there is no love, not for the Earth, not for each other, and not for one's self.

So many of my psychotherapy clients speak of feeling "dead" inside. They explain how money, success, and possessions don't seem to assuage the emptiness in their spirits. They do not feel truly alive, but rather like automatons moving through space and time to the click of programmed existence.

It is perhaps no coincidence that May, when spring is at its height, frequently has more suicides than any other month of the year. The sight of life bursting anew may, by contrast, intensify the deadness that lays waste to the desperate soul. Perhaps when the Earth is resplendent in new life, her alienated children most acutely experience their spiritual homelessness.

On a recent flight to New York, I saw this deadness in a less drastic but still telling instance.

As we approached the coast of the Atlantic Ocean, there was a towering thunderhead off to our south. The sun was well down, but the tops of the clouds glowed softly with a bluish-pink tint. Waves of low scud clouds encircled the pillar of the storm, rising to it like foothills toward an alpine peak. Inside the thunderstorm, which rose well over 45,000 feet, lightning shot its tendrils again and again, igniting the clouds in bright relief against the dark backdrop of the night sky. We descended and banked north to skirt the storm, but still our path took us close in. The plane lowered into a deep valley between the main thunderhead and a secondary wall of lesser but still towering clouds, and we slipped through like a bird gliding in a mountainous valley, an atmospheric fjord.

It was, by any measure, spectacular. Or so I thought.

When I looked around at the other passengers, I realized none within my sight were watching the majesty just outside our windows. They were absorbed in magazines, in-flight movies, novels, and paper-thin conversation, while within a flick of their eyes the sky was a display of sacred majesty. Perhaps some were afraid of this display of nature's undeniable power, while others may simply have failed to appreciate the natural splendor around them.

These days, far too many of us suffer this blindness, either out of fear or the absence of awareness. Like the orphaned child, we do not recognize our own Mother when she stands before us.

We walk past her as if she is a ghost.

Yet we are the dead ones.

EXERCISE:

CEREMONY OF RE-AWAKENING

Waking up from our perceptual deadness toward the Earth requires only a brief ceremony repeated as needed. Our awareness is shaped by what we choose to pay attention to. "You are what you think, having become what you thought," is how Gautama Buddha purportedly phrased this truth. When we focus our attention primarily on human-made things and activities, our consciousness of nature diminishes accordingly. Simply by attending to aspects of our Earth Mother, we stir her life force within ourselves, and we gradually awaken from the living dead of consciousness-alienated-from-life.

- Identify an object or location in nature that attracts your attention and appreciation. This could be as close as your own back yard, a nearby park, a tree outside your bedroom window—any thing or place that seems to "speak" to you.
- "Shine" your awareness on this object or location. For a few minutes, illuminate it with your senses by looking, listening, smelling, and touching.
- For several consecutive days, return to study this same object or place, and each time seek to notice some other aspect of it that previously escaped your observation.
- As you seek to exhaust your awareness of this object or place, pay attention to the tremendous variations and subtleties that each of your senses can perceive in it. For example, the "seeing" of something can occur at the macro level (perceiving an object or scene as a whole – the big picture) or micro level (noticing the parts that comprise the whole). In addition, seeing can be divided into brightness, variations in color and hue, shifting between foreground and background, shadows, patterns, and so on.
- Continue your contemplations with the same natural object or location until you are certain you have exhausted all the elements and nuances available to you through your senses. This can take a long time. Because so much in nature is ever-changing, one could probably spend a

lifetime watching a tree grow, for instance.

- When you do shift from one object or location to another, seek contrast. For example, if your first focus is an animal or beach (a rapidly changing entity), consider selecting a less energetic object for your next focus, such as a rock or tree trunk. You may be surprised to discover that even so-called "inert" objects are full of life, and that it is our perception of them that creates the illusion of their deadness.

- Some people elect to create an indoor "nature table" where they place various natural objects—moss, rocks, shells, leaves, dried flowers, and so on. They use these for their ceremonial meditations. Placing a nature table in a child's room is particularly useful method for sustaining that youngster's sense of bonding with the Earth, as well. In selecting items for a nature table, please be respectful of the environment. Do not take things that are being used by other creatures (bird nests, for instance), that are critical to an ecosystem, or whose absence will detract from the enjoyment of others.

We do not bring nature to life, nature brings us to life. By drinking in the Earth's life through our senses, we enliven our own souls. This rejuvenation is available to each of us every day. Even those who live in densely populated, urban areas can find pockets of nature in their midst, and these can serve as oases that re-awaken one's sensitivity to life.

ALIVENESS

*We shall not cease from exploration
And the end of all our exploring
Will be to arrive where we started
And know the place for the first time.*

Poet T. S. Eliot

Despite the perceptual deadness and apathy toward the natural world that many of us suffer, there is an ember that burns in our souls, and it can reignite the flame of life that the native peoples often called "the sacred fire." This spiritual spark most often manifests itself in our emotions, even those we find uncomfortable or painful. What we consider common feelings offer us a hallowed conduit back toward the life force, even when these feelings seem to torment us.

Human emotions are some of the most confusing and inexplicable "whatevers" that have ever refused to submit to rational analysis, yet they are what make us feel alive. Why we feel the way we do, what our feelings mean, how we should cope with them, and what their purpose is remain largely unanswered questions despite an endless flood of psychological research and on-the-couch analysis. Our emotional lives seem an enigma, but not so much as we may imagine.

39

Our feelings can help return us home, and that may well be one of their primary purposes—to provide the clues that help us rediscover our origins in the life force. They are signposts along nature's way. Even those emotions that leave us feeling lost, such as anger, sadness, and guilt, can be spiritual markers that allow us to track the workings of the life force in our own psyches, eventually leading us home to heal.

On the surface, our emotions do not seem to possess so lofty a purpose. Even when we label our feelings, assign causes, and suggest how to act in response to them, they bedevil us, demonstrating how little control we have over our inner lives. We don't wake up in the morning and say, "Gosh, I think I'll be depressed today." Depression, like happiness, anger, love, fear, and all the rest, happens to us. And despite all the neatly packaged pop psychology that promises mastery over our emotions, few if any of us attain such power. Even the widely prescribed mood-altering drugs, such as tranquilizers, sleeping potions, and anti-depressants, do not control our emotions, but merely modulate their intensities.

From where most of us sit, emotions seem to get in our way, not show us the way.

Consequently, many of us are seduced by control strategies that promise us mastery over our emotions. Psychoactive medications, psychotherapy, self-help and support groups, meditation, nutritional and exercise regimens, religious and New Age cults—all are popular by virtue of their promises of emotional change, ostensibly for the better. Call it what you will—peace of mind, self-actualization, enlightenment, getting high, getting off, getting god—the lure is essentially singular.

Make me feel better. Give me control. Get these feelings under my thumb or out of my way.

Some of these methods deliver to some degree. People who go to AA meetings, take Prozac, join religious communities, practice transcendental meditation, do Tai Chi, or go on a Zen macrobiotic diet are likely to experience mood changes, including positive ones. But the essential elements of emotional life (change and unpredictability) do not disappear. None of us has the power to willfully direct our feeling existence.

That is because our emotions are not entirely our own.

Experiences like sadness, joy, anxiety, and contentment are natural and innate. They are part of our nature, and that nature is derived from the substance and spirit of the life force. Emotions are the workings of this life force within each of us, and they have much to do with that equally mysterious phenomenon known as "the will to live" which, when in decline, leads to illness and death.

When you experience your feelings, you are sensing the changes and energies of the life force within your own individual being. Emotions are energy in motion. Depression, as an example, is one manifestation of our life energy, a manifestation that is deep, dark, slow, and listless, and which most of us consider unpleasant at best. There are many analogous displays of depression (as a kind of energy in motion) in nature outside of the human realm. The overcast or foggy day, the still and tepid pond, the oppressive heat of a windless afternoon, the depth of winter, the dark of earliest morning, the ailing plant or animal, the aftermath of a damaging storm—all are exhibitions of the depressive quality of life's many energies.

The Earth did not evolve the depressive aspect of the life force in order to torment itself or its creatures. As is true with physical and chemical processes, emotional contrasts and opposites support and facilitate each other. Happiness, for instance, is dependent upon sadness for its existence. Like it or not, there is no love without hate, and no compassion without anger. "Peaks require valleys," the adage goes.

Nature's way—whether in humans or in the natural environment—is robustly emotional and oscillating with contrast.

Human beings did not invent emotions. We merely labeled them. Labeling is an activity we sometimes employ to keep our feelings at an intellectual arm's length. But labeled or merely felt, emotions are part of nature and, in varying configurations and degrees, are inherent in all living entities. "Living" is defined here in the broadest possible sense. The wind, for instance, is quite alive despite popular notions to the contrary. Clearly it harbors moods. The angry tempest, the content calm, the loving warmth of a summer night's breeze, and the depressing bite of the winter wind all reflect the emotional character of natural processes. Like our moods, all the "moods" of the wind are emotion—energy in motion.

Some will argue that assigning feeling states to nature is but one more example of human arrogance and projection. "Nature just is, objectively, and we are the ones who try to assign it meanings it does not possess," a colleague of mine contends. Perhaps, but this seems an empty and likewise arrogant position, one which places the source of meaning in people, not in the natural world, and which denies that the Earth Mother is an entity in her own right.

Feelings are not exclusive to people, but rather reflect our participation in the larger emotional life of the planet.

My premise is that we derive our emotional, psychological, and spiritual nature from our Earth Mother, not the other way around. We are not separate from her, and so our lives are an extension and expression of her collective life. We are the parts that help give expression to her as a whole. We have emotions because nature is emotional, and because we are inside of nature, not outside of it. We have a spiritual life because the Earth is a numinous entity, a manifestation in the material realm of spiritual energy, a fact recently rediscovered by quantum physicists but long ago understood by native peoples throughout the globe.

We may learn how to act and think, what to believe, and how to behave from our human families and social communities, but the raw materials of our emotional lives come from our home in nature. In the workings of the Earth we can visibly observe and experience the nuances of feeling that, within ourselves, seem so invisible, mysterious, and confusing. Emotions bind us to our Mother, and if we are lost from her, they offer a way back.

Terry illustrates this reality. When he trudged into my office, he was

41

as depressed as he had ever been in his 30-some years. With the American Dream tucked firmly under his belt, he could see no reason to be so downcast, yet he was. Terry wanted to talk things through, so we spent our initial counseling sessions doing just that. As with many of us, all his mouth aerobics did little to enlighten or uplift him, and our discussions failed to uncover obvious causes for his despair. Both of us felt medication was not the way to go, so I suggested a truly natural course of treatment.

"Here are the directions to my parents' farm," I said, handing him a crudely drawn map. "Nobody will hassle you. Just go there, park the car next to the barn, and walk due north along the tractor path. The ponds are about three-quarters of a mile away at the back of the property, surrounded by a stand of trees."

"What good will this do?" he protested.

"Trust me, but dress very warm. The land is quite flat, and in January there's no protection from the wind. Insulated boots, warm gloves, and a hat are a must," I cautioned.

"This makes me feel pretty silly," he said.

"That's an improvement already. Silly feels better than glum."

As Terry reported to me later, the afternoon sky was steel gray when he stepped from his car onto the snow-packed crust beside the barn. The brisk wind slapped him on the face. He didn't feel comfortable, but he felt alive.

He worried that the sky promised snow, but pulled on his gloves and oriented himself to the farm's geography. Then he was off, head down, plodding through the whiteness, out into the flat, snow-covered fields. Within minutes his cadence had settled into a heavy-stepped staccato. It was tough going, he told me later, but then so is life.

As is customary for someone mired in depression, Terry paid little heed to his immediate surroundings. He was far off in some cognitive tar pit, mired in his repetitive and bleak thoughts, and the more he struggled to yank loose, the tighter he stuck. One cannot *think* one's way out of sadness. In fact, it's pretty hard to deeply understand the nature of what we call "depression" (a modern, sterile term for sadness) or any other primary emotion through rational analysis. Thinking is just too abstract and ungrounded to provide the where-you-live understanding that emotions require, which is why I urged Terry out into the snow.

Terry said that before long he found it difficult to continue thinking about being depressed. In fact, it grew tougher to think about anything. The frigid wind, the heavy footfalls, and the glaring whiteness stirred up enough sensory input to overload all the mental chatter that we euphemistically call "thinking." In short order, the elements turned Terry into a sensing animal immersed in a difficult habitat, rather than a cerebral computer churning out self-absorbed thoughts.

"This may sound a bit dramatic, but it got to be a struggle. I wasn't sure I had the stamina to tough it out," Terry told me later.

But he did, and upon reaching the wind buffer of the trees, Terry plopped down on the trunk of a fallen birch whose top branches were encased in the ice of the frozen pond. The clouds had lowered some, and with the wind veering to the southeast, snow seemed imminent. But snow or not, Terry had an assignment to complete.

He pulled the small notebook from his coat pocket. On the first page he found three questions I had asked him to jot down and answer. "What is alive? What is dead? What is the difference?"

Terry started with the tree that served as his bench.

"I told myself that the tree I was sitting on was dead, that was for sure," he reported to me. "And I figured I would be, too, if I took too long to answer your questions."

Suddenly, he told me, something grabbed at his awareness, the way insights do just before they burst through the curtains of the subconscious mind and step on-stage. Something was, as we say, on the tip of his tongue. And as he struggled to decipher the hieroglyphics in his head, his gaze drifted out across the snow.

"There was something about the snow," he told me. "It covered everything with cold. The pond and the fish and frogs, and the larva under the ice. And it buried the grass and the ground where the worms and snakes were—but they weren't dead. They were just sleeping."

Terry said he sat there awhile wondering about all this, not quite certain how to piece it together or even why it mattered to him, but also sensing its significance, certain that he would do well to understand what lay before him. He peered out at the cloak of snow for as far as he could see, and noticed how it seemed like a blanket pulled over all the inert, hibernating life underneath. "Sleeping," he mumbled to himself, and then a few flakes lighted on his arm. The snow, the blanket, was falling on him also, he realized. With that, he told me, the pencil in his gloved hand fell away, and all his musings quickly became quite clear.

"I realized that my depression is like the snow. It covers everything in me, and it's like my heart has gone to sleep, like the life in me is sleeping," he told me. "But I'm not dead inside. I'm resting."

Sitting there in the snow, Terry said he saw an image in his head of what to do next, and rather than analyzing, censoring, or denigrating it, he took a chance. He followed and trusted the image. This was quite a departure from his customary approach. His mind was inclined to surgically dissect his feelings. But then, visions can do that to people—they jar us out of old, repetitive ways.

The next thing he knew, Terry was down in the snow, burrowing as best he could into a drift on the edge of the pond, covering himself, burying himself in the cold whiteness. And the sky began to spit snow, helping him somehow, it seemed to him.

"I've never done anything so irrational in my life," he later told me.

"I doubt that," I replied. "You just don't remember all those crazy things you did as a little kid."

"Maybe. Anyway, there I was burying myself in the snow."

"And what was that like?" I asked.

"I kept saying to myself, 'I'm alive,' over and over, and it felt like I was becoming that part of me that the depression hasn't killed, the part of me that still lives under the depression, under the snow," he said, straining to explain his feelings.

Terry looked out my office window at the winter sky.

"I guess this sounds pretty crazy, huh?" He sought some reassurance.

"Actually, it sounds extremely sane," I replied. "You discovered the truth about your sadness; that it is putting something inside you to sleep, like the snow puts the land and plants and many animals to sleep."

With that Terry began to cry a little.

"While I was under the snow, I felt warm. It sounds weird, but I felt warm and alive . . . and waiting," he said.

"Waiting for what?" I asked.

"For spring. I'm waiting for my spring, to wake up, to come back," he half whispered through his tears.

"And you will," I added. "As sure as the Spring. You will."

The Earth did not cure Terry in some stunning display of ecological revelation. Rather, it put before him a mirror, and in it he perceived his emotional reflection and saw his heart clearly for the first time. The understanding that nature afforded him cannot be captured in thought, or in the words on this page, for like the natural world itself, the Earth's wisdom will not be constrained by our intellects. Instead, it gave Terry the sort of understanding that is felt-knowledge, the knowing of babies yet unborn, of owls seeing in utter blackness, of winds shaping the sands for millions of years, of seeds waiting for the season's call, of caribou bound for the calving grounds, of clouds making rain from dust and vapor. And in this unique way of witnessing, he comprehended his malady.

"For the first time in a long while, I make sense to me," Terry concluded. "I understand what this sadness is about. I can't put it into words very well, but deep down, I understand."

"Stay with that," I counseled. "It will take you where you need to go next. Don't worry about the words or the concepts. Follow the feeling. In that feeling you will find nature's way . . . your way."

"I still don't know exactly what happened to me under that snow," he muttered. "I just know something did."

"Neither do I," I replied. "But our Mother knows, and if you stay with her, she'll show you someday."

If we are to deeply grasp and assimilate the meanings of our emotions and allow them to be the transformative forces in our lives that they truly can be, then we must return to their source, and to our source—the Earth. Like water evaporated from the sea, condensed into clouds, and rained back upon the land, our feelings seek their wellspring in nature, flowing back in the rivers of joy, sadness, love, and anger that run through our hearts. If we follow them back to the Earth and seek them there instead of in our mental menageries, we shall regain the aliveness that modern culture has drained from our souls.

In our feelings, we are not alone.

The Earth is with us.

EXERCISE:

CEREMONY OF FEELING

Modern psychology encourages us to comprehend our emotional lives through the vehicle of intellectual understanding. But emotions are not born of our intellects. They are manifestations of the larger feeling life of nature, of which each of us is a part. Emotions are not concepts, they are experiences. If you don't believe that, then you've never had one. You can attain a more profound and transformative understanding of your emotions.

- Identify a feeling you want to work with. It doesn't need to be problematic or painful, although those sorts of emotions are appropriate, as well.
- Next, answer these questions about your feeling:
1. What plant, animal, or object in nature comes closest to depicting my emotion?
2. What natural process is similar to my emotion?
3. If my feeling were a time of day, when would it be?
4. If my feeling were a type of weather, what would it be?
- From your answers to these questions, determine what thing or process in nature most clearly represents the emotion you want to work with.
- Next, determine how you can observe or interact with this natural thing or process.
- Some folks find it helpful to record this entire process in a "feelings journal." This allows the intellect to share in the heart's deeper understanding of your emotional life.

Example: One young man I counseled wanted to transform his volatile anger. The analogy he found in nature was in violent thunderstorms. Recognizing there were some dangers involved, he nonetheless elected to go out in these storms and immerse himself in their sound and fury. Eventually, he allowed himself to "act out" his anger through the fury of such storms, largely by screaming with the thunder, howling with the wind, and braving the heavy rain.

45

Example: A middle-aged client of mine wanted to deal with her shame, a prevalent feeling state. The analogy in nature which she identified for her shame was "the kill" (any predator dispatching its prey). For her, shame resulted from her perception that in taking care of her own needs, she often had to put others second, or even offend them. She closely observed predatory relationships in nature, either directly or on film. At first, she found this witnessing process quite agonizing, but gradually her perception of the predatory interaction changed. It seemed more natural and necessary. While not a "predator" in her relationships with other people, she recognized the necessity of attending to her own needs at times, and she no longer felt ashamed of doing so.

Our individual emotional experiences are joined with the larger, collective feeling life of the Earth. Emotions in isolation, cut off from their source and meaning in nature, can be ruinous and destructive. By linking our feelings with their wellsprings in the Earth, we reconstitute our sacred bond of emotion.

NATURE'S TYPOLOGY

There is no place to seek the mind;
It is like the footprints of the birds in the sky.

Buddhist Monk Zenrin

I guess the birds showed me.
A crow, actually.

Maybe that's because birds have been around so long and so successfully, beginning as dinosaurs and then, in the hot fires of some evolutionary cataclysm, transforming themselves into creatures that ply our Mother's atmospheric ocean, the sky. Perhaps it stems from their tremendous variety, paradoxically coupled with their amazing similarity. All birds are fundamentally alike, yet each type is vastly different.

Kind of like people.

I was in a twilight sleep in our rented cabin on a northern Minnesota lake. The night's memory of a loon's eerie cries still reverberated in my consciousness that early morning, but the crows made short work of that. One planted itself just outside the window and proceeded to "caw" with that sharp, abrasive cackle that distinguishes crows from their more melodious cousins. The sound sliced through what remained of my sleep, and I opened my eyes to see the dawn's swelling radiance slipping through the curtains.

In a few seconds another crow answered the first bird's call, but it was a ways off, down by the shore. Several of them went on like this, cawing in sequence, the farther ones sounding like echoes of the nearest. When it was clear that their discussion would not permit me to return to my slumber, I went to the window to pinpoint the instigator of all the racket.

The nearest crow sat on a picnic table a few yards from the window, and when I pulled open the curtains, it gave me a quick look before taking flight, cawing all the way. Staggering into the living room and plopping on the spongy couch, I got to wondering about crows, about how their personalities are unique among the birds.

It was the word "personalities" that grabbed me.

We humans use it repeatedly in reference to that matrix of attitudes, temperaments, and behaviors that forms the personhood of each individual. When we speak of someone's personality, we are attempting to describe the essence of who she or he is, coining labels such as "outgoing" or "introverted," "cold" or "warm," and many others. Mental health professionals, like myself, employ the term more specifically, using it to describe certain kinds of psychological diagnoses, such as obsessive-compulsive personality, narcissistic personality, and borderline personality.

The word—personality—suggests that only persons have these defining characteristics, but that just isn't so. As with emotions, the quality of personality is everywhere evident in nature, not just in our species.

It was clear to me then, even in my morning mental fog, that crows have a personality quite distinct from loons, eagles, hummingbirds, pigeons, or most any other sort of bird. They possess a core of emotive and behavioral attributes that gives us a feeling for who they are as distinct creatures.

This is no revelation, even to modern folks. Pet owners, for example, are intensely familiar with the concept of personalities in animals. Dogs, cats, parakeets, guppies, and ferrets each have unique emotional qualities. These are not simply qualities we project onto them in an act of personification, but those that are their own and that draw humans to desire contact with them.

Native Americans were inherently conscious of this phenomenon, believing that animals, plants, topographical elements, and even natural events possess emotional and spiritual characteristics. Many Native Americans' names reflected this recognition—Standing Bear, Little Crow, Red Cloud, Sitting Bull, Thunder Heart, Crazy Horse, and countless others. Their cultures realized that personality is not derived from persons, but rather is an aspect of the natural world that manifests itself in humans, animals, plants, mountains, rivers, and other guises and faces of the Earth.

We do not give ourselves personalities. We are *given* personalities. Ask any parent. Each child is born with an innate temperament, an essential emotional disposition, and a response pattern toward life. This core personality is the foundation upon which acquired traits collect. Opinions, values, and nuances of behavior coalesce around each person's core personality much like rings of growth in a tree, or layers of ice around a speck of dust that is the nucleus of a hail stone. But each individual's central essence is not created by family, parenting, or experiences. It is created by our Earth Mother.

At the urging of modern psychology, most of us have sought to understand ourselves, our personalities, by delving into our decidedly human characteristics. We study and explore the human family, the developmental effects of childhood experiences, the impact of genetic and neurochemical influences, life stages, and other shapers of personhood. By examining these concepts, we are told, one can grow to understand one's self, one's personality.

But this is far from the whole picture.

Personality extends well beyond the human species. When we speak of someone's personality we are, after all, referring to her or his spirit, that unseen but deeply felt essence that is the unique expression of a single life. And while certain behaviors and attitudes are a reflection of developmental influences, a person's spirit is also a representation of her or his source: the Earth.

Our Mother manifests her disposition in countless variations, from the dark to the divine; from the spider that paralyzes, cocoons, and sucks its victims dry to the person who lays down her or his life to save another. Hers is not a singular personality type, but rather all the wondrous varieties that we see around us in the natural world: cruel and compassionate, quiet and uproarious, secretive and exposed, joyous and despairing, slow and swift, brave and cowering, beautiful and ugly, creative and robotic, forthright and deceptive. Just as violets, glorious sunsets, peacocks, and a beautiful child are expressions of the Earth's penchant for loveliness, so scorpions, volcanoes, stinkweed, and tornadoes are manifestations of her shadowy side, at least from our narrow human perspective.

I often ask psychotherapy clients to simplify long and rambling descriptions of their basic personalities by identifying an animal, plant, or natural element or process that expresses the essence of who they are. Most accomplish this assignment with relative ease.

"I'm an otter," a nine-year-old boy told me, his parents nodding in immediate agreement.

"How so?" I asked.

"I'm quick, I like to play, and I eat a lot," he replied.

"And he gets into a lot of mischief," his father added.

"Sounds like an otter to me," I concluded.

Innately we understand that nature is resplendent with personality types, and we perceive the obvious similarities between our own personalities and those of the creatures and life processes that surround us. We may imagine that our personalities are "deeper" or "more complex" than those found in birds, trees, waves, or tundra, but this merely reflects our penchant for hubris. We humans have done a fine job of complicating the phenomenon of personality, but not of understanding it.

"What aspect of nature best symbolizes your husband's personality?" I asked a woman during a marriage counseling session.

"The ocean," she responded, without a moment's contemplation.

"Why an ocean?" her husband asked.

"Because you're so changeable. One moment you're calm and inviting, and the next all hell breaks loose. Then I'm just struggling to keep my head above water," she explained.

"What's she like?" I asked him, trying to be fair and square.

"A Venus flytrap," he replied.

"I beg your pardon!" she said.

"You're sweet, but once I get inside, look out!"

Obviously, things didn't turn out well for these two, and while their respective descriptions were deeply influenced by how they felt toward each other at the time, both readily perceived how personality is an attribute of nature. Later, when I asked each of them alone to describe their own personalities by using an example from nature, they offered very different analogies. He saw himself as a house cat—aloof, cunning, agile, and capable of affection, but only on his own terms. She thought of herself as a rose—delicate, but with a protective exterior she created to defend herself from what she perceived as his emotional hostility.

In contrast to personality, moods can change rapidly. Someone who is sullen one hour can turn jubilant the next. Personality is more stable over time. It is like the deep current below the sea's swiftly changing surface. In the depths of one's being, there is a more steady flow, while closer to the exterior emotional changes come and go with the vagaries of the wind.

It is our deep personality that is given to each of us by our Earth Mother. In it we find her imprint and one of our closest links with the wellspring of our nature. When we identify creatures, objects, or processes in the natural world that resemble us in personality, we are afforded the opportunity to glean who we are in the deepest psychological and spiritual sense. Other animals, plants, mountains, rivers, rocks, and clouds—all are like mirrors in which we can see and study ourselves.

Again, Native Americans practicing traditional ways retain a firm sense of this connection. Their belief that each human has a "spirit animal" and that all things in nature possess a spiritual essence reflects their recognition that our individual personalities are mirrored in the flora, fauna, and actions of the Earth. One's spirit animal is an expression of one's fundamental nature, which can also be recognized in another creature. In Native American traditions, the spirit animal is a source of communication with the life force, a conduit back through the spiritual umbilical to the Earth.

Regrettably, modern culture in America does not embrace the notion of a spirit animal, or the idea that personality is an implicit aspect of nature. So when I suggest to a client that she or he might better understand the deepest self by observing its reflection in the natural world, that person frequently questions the sanity of this therapist.

One fellow I worked with was uncommonly open to this suggestion. He saw his nature in a large hunk of granite, one he had labored long and hard to dig up when he was a child on the family farm. In psychological terms he was a reserved, introverted fellow, very consistent in his moods, solid and dependable. Nonetheless, he was troubled by feeling "kind of dead inside," as he put it. Because he was a cautious and conventional person, and an accountant by trade, I hardly expected him to embrace the personality-in-nature notion, but he took right to it. At my urging, he agreed to acquire the old granite rock from his father's farm.

Returning it to the backyard of his suburban home, he complied with my suggestion that he spend time observing and studying the granite each day, in an effort to perceive his personality within it. As one would expect, he made an accounting of these observations, recording them in an orderly ledger.

"I was surprised," he reported after a few weeks of study. "There's much more to a hunk of granite than I imagined."

"Like what?" I asked.

"It's intricate. I noticed the way the constituent elements of stone are fused into a whole rock, and the different colors, and how they reflect light. It's more than just a clump."

"And what about you?" I asked.

"That's true about me, too. From a distance, or if you just give me a passing glance, I look like any other person—any other stone, so to speak. But if you take the time to study me, I have a lot of facets," he replied.

"Anything else?"

"While I'm solid and don't change much, I blend in with other living things pretty well. So does the granite. It has grass growing around it, and some moss is starting to grow on it. Animals come and sit on it and seem to like it. The other morning, I saw a baby bunny resting under one corner of the rock in the shade."

"What does that have to do with you?"

"I'm that way, too. People who seem more alive and more outgoing collect around me, and they seem to feel safe with me, even protected by me. I seem to help others that way, just by being there, by being who I am," he said.

All this from a rock? Was this guy just projecting like crazy, using the rock as a kind of inkblot? Could he just as easily have seen himself in a rhinoceros, an oak, or an icicle? Maybe, but he intuitively identified with the granite. Something in his own deeper consciousness recognized the kinship he felt with that specific expression of the Earth. And in a thing that most of us do not perceive as alive, he experienced living forces very similar to those working in his own deepest nature.

Nature speaks volumes to us about who we are. The best lenses for seeing ourselves are rarely found in psychological theories and their descriptive terminologies. While we can build theoretical houses made of mental cards with all our labels and psychodynamic explanations, they lack the solid simplicity afforded by the Earth's analogies.

Now, instead of asking my clients to describe their personalities with terms like "introverted" or "sensitive" or "moody," I present questions, such as:

"What season are you like?"

"If you were a month, which one would you be?"

"What time of day are you?"

"Is there an animal, plant, or object in nature that is a lot like you?"

"What sort of topography matches your inner landscape?"

"What kind of weather best illustrates your personality?"

When a client, or a friend for that matter, feels the urge to illuminate her or his deeper self, I urge that person to turn to the Earth. The mirror of understanding is more likely to be found there than in a self-help book, a navel-gazing talk show, or several grand worth of psychoanalysis.

Like one's human mother, the Earth Mother knows the nature of her child.

If we ask, look, and listen, she will reveal that nature to us.

Like Mother, like child.

EXERCISE:

CEREMONY OF PERSONALITY

Within the natural world, personality is everywhere evident and resplendent with variation. As direct expressions of this world, our personalities are paralleled by the "personalities" found in natural processes, creatures, and objects. You can employ the Earth as a mirror to more clearly perceive your own nature.

- Begin by recalling any natural object, process, animal, or plant for which you have always felt a strong, spontaneous affinity.
- Answering these questions may help:
1. What animal, plant, object, or natural process most closely resembles my personality?
2. Is there a time of day that feels like my personality? Some of us feel we are "a morning person," for example.
3. What season of the year feels most like my personality?
4. Is there a type of topography that seems to reflect my inner landscape? Are you, as examples, more like a desert, mountain, seashore, or prairie?
5. What kind of weather resembles my inner atmosphere?
- Once you identify your personality counterpart in nature, seek it out, either directly in the natural world (if this is possible) or through books, or audio or video media. By contemplating this natural object, process, or entity, you can determine if it truly does constitute a clarifying reflection of your personality.
- While it may seem a romantic notion, in my experience not all people are able to identify a "spirit animal" in this regard. But most can determine some aspect of nature that speaks to their inner constitution, their core personality.

Example: A middle-aged man I counseled felt that he was experiencing a "mid-life crisis." For the first time in many years, he found himself introspectively examining his emotional and spiritual nature, and yet he was confused and unable to perceive his basic personality. He had read many books on the subject of life transition and stages, but none seemed helpful. At my urging, he sought a personality template in nature and soon found it in the clouds. Like them, he experienced himself as ever-changing, always moving, and shaped and driven by unseen forces greater than himself. He meditated almost daily on the clouds, began photographing them, and he studied their names and meteorological significance. The clouds became a defining motif of his inner life—one which gave him a blue-print for understanding his own inner being and place in nature. When he became confused about himself, he turned to the clouds and, through them, he felt a deep comprehension and compassion for his own nature.

We strive to understand our personality through the forms and processes of our Earth. While not turning away entirely from intellectual comprehension, we seek to deeply embrace a more intuitive and heartfelt cognizance of who we are.

RHYTHM OF LIFE

The great sea
Has sent me adrift
It moves me
As the weed in a great river
Earth and the great weather
Move me
Have carried me away
And move my inward parts with joy.

Inuit Shaman Uvavnuk

"Just go sit," Florence, my older sister, insisted.

"What am I, a dog?" I quipped.

"Sit . . . just sit." She pointed toward the beach, and then walked into the cabin, pausing to dip her sandy feet in a bucket of water at the door.

I turned toward my appointed destination. The water was but a few yards away, behind a low sand dune tufted with intermittent beach grass like a balding head. A very brisk southeasterly was blowing up the Lake Michigan shore, and the breaking rollers on the leeward side pummeled the sand in rapid succession. But the beach effortlessly absorbed all the water's bending blows.

The duet of wind and surfing waves raised a two-part chorus of white noise—that diffuse, fuzzy fizz of sound that lulls the cerebral cortex like a mother's breath does a sleeping babe.

But I was anything but lulled.

The weeks preceding my visit to the beach for a family reunion had been relentless, avalanche-like, rapid-fire. I was as close to stressed-out as I'd ever been, and it showed. My eyes and face had that cavernous shadow that simultaneously cries "Let me out of here, but I'm too tired to run." I felt none of the peace, connection, and steadfastness that I preached to my clients, and the idea of being bonded with my Earth Mother had begun to seem like some hypocritical joke—one I had perpetrated upon myself as well as those who trusted me to help them with emotional healing.

For me it was a time of disharmony, when the rhythms of my life were bereft of any sustainable cadence. All the "sounds" of my existence had become discordant, chaotic mish-mash.

At some point or other, all of us feel this emotional stuttering. It is the opposite of feeling "in synch" and "in the groove." There is no ease to living. Everything is an effort, and the more one tries, the more dissonant life becomes. One feels unnatural.

Modern life has a talent for getting us into this fumble-bumble state. The light-speed pace of daily doings, the multiplicity of demands, the immediacy of expectations and needs, the juggling of what once would have been considered three or four lives on the pinpoint of a single existence—these and other insanities rob us of what 60s folks used to call "going with the flow." Subject yourself to enough of the current modus operandi, and there is no flow, just a flash flood down a rocky canyon.

As aspiring lyricist Shawn Colvin put it, "I'm riding shotgun down an avalanche."

Such was the state of my existence.

Despite my sorry condition, I had a dozen reasons not to just sit, even if my older sister had so commanded. I had a newspaper column to finish, several letters to write, phone calls back to my office, a client to check on, and something else I just had to do but couldn't remember.

Despite these tuggings, I made the wiser choice. I just sat.

My bottom wiggled into the sand, forming its own chair. I experienced nature's perfect fit, contoured exactly to one's shape, weight, and density. A yard from my toes, the waves reached their farthest advance toward the land, then fell away, the sand hissing as it drank them in. The wind, curling hard in advance of a storm front, pushed into my face and whistled across my ears. Before me, the Earth composed a song. Nature offered the steady ebb and flow of the waves, the graceful refrain of the wind, the clouds dancing through the sky, the sands shifting and shaping, the sea grass willowing before the invisible pluckings and strummings of the air. The synchronization was magnificent, as it always is in nature.

By sitting in the midst of this symphony, I gradually became a part of it, another instrument that, by my simple presence, blended with the others. Unknowingly, I began to rock ever so slightly, merging with the physical percussions around me. Then a low humming with a chant-like measure rose from my chest and throat. A sense of rhythm and congruence seeped back into my soul. I was flowing again.

From these ancient, primordial rhythms we have derived our human versions of "music," both the auditory variety and that which is purely emotional. Music was not invented when some long-ago composer decided to blow through a hollow reed or tap an empty seed pod. It began long before our species. The Earth has been composing music for eons. Our modern versions, even those produced by synthesizers and electrified instruments, all are based upon nature's sense of rhythm, harmonics, tone, and cadence.

Tribal cultures understood this. Their dances, as one example, are infused with the movements, sounds, and harmonies of the natural music. Their songs and choreographies are direct expressions of the Earth's: of animals running together through a field of flowing grass, the grass itself in rapport with the wind; of waters chorusing over rocks like a thousand fingers on piano keys; of howls and bird songs; of rain spattering on a still pond and booming thunder; of crickets calls and the hiss of snow racing across a frozen lake. These are compositions of the most basic and yet extraordinary sort. Their variety is infinite, and they're never out of tune.

Because we are extensions of the natural world, we, too, are creatures of rhythm and cycle.

In working with someone in psychotherapy, I attempt to assess her or his emotional rhythms, those psychological and spiritual resonances that convey the feeling of being in natural flow or, inversely, of being anomalous, or out of whack. After many years of doing this, I have come to define people as being (1) in a state of "flow," (2) in a condition of "discord," or (3) in one of "blocking."

While in flow, one's emotions, behaviors, and thoughts are dancing in synch, like three partners moving to the same beat and not tripping over each other. This is not necessarily an enjoyable state. One can be flowing in a state of sadness, anger, or fear, as well as flowing in happiness or excitement. But whatever one's situation, while in flow, feelings, thoughts, and actions are moving in harmony.

Discord is the obvious opposite. Here, for example, someone may be emotionally sad but pretending to be happy, and all the while thinking, "I shouldn't be sad." There is no congruence between actions, thoughts, and emotions, so the messages are garbled and stuttered. Emotional music becomes mere dissonant noise.

In a blocking condition, there is neither flow nor disjointed discord. Rather, one is shut down, trying not to feel. It's an attempt to find shelter in a psychological coma. Inert. Static. Sometimes, blocking is an effort to freeze painful or frightening feelings, a kind of desperate defense, like a stun gun used on one's heart. It rarely persists for long. Like the river that is blocked, our feelings try to dig a hole, overflow, or erode the barrier. Then, in human terms, we develop symptoms: depression, panic attacks, tension headaches, heart attacks, and so on.

Unlike some of her human progeny, the Earth Mother flows, though not always happily. Her storms, floods, earthquakes, and mosquito population booms are not wonderful experiences, but they flow.

She exhibits a harmonious relationship in all her parts and processes. Her dance, even if disastrous for some of her creatures, is not chaotic or discordant.

When we, as children of our Mother, grow out of synch within ourselves, we can regain a real, sensory experience of harmony by visiting the natural world. Again, through the avenues of our senses, we can observe the flowing dance of the Mother and join it.

Alternatively, one can spend tons of time and money talking to someone like me about how discombobulated one feels. And while insight is valuable, it doesn't necessarily change anything. The conclusion of many therapy sessions that examine emotional disharmony is the profound conclusion that "I'm messed up, all right." Important to know, but not necessarily useful for altering one's condition.

Granted, an hour of sensory tuning-in at the beach, by the stream, under the shade tree, on the nature trail, or atop the wind-swept butte won't fix all the broken stuff in our lives, but it will pull us out of our writhing minds and into our grounded, flowing senses. It encourages us to dance and prance with the Earth's melodies.

That will nurture the experience of inner flow. And when we re-enter the unnatural world that tripped us up to begin with, the inner flow may help keep our emotions, thoughts, and behaviors playing in tune.

What's so wonderful about being in a state of flow, aside from the fact that it sounds nice and has a New Age ring to it? Plenty. Flow takes us where we need to go, toward the next step in our psychological and spiritual journey. It is part of nature's way of healing.

For instance, someone who is afraid but attempting not to show it, who tries to appear unruffled, generally experiences what is called "anxiety." He or she is like a driver with one foot flooring the accelerator and the other rammed down on the brake pedal. Inside, this person feels the customary emotional and physical manifestations of fear—the churning stomach, the rapidly beating heart, and breathlessness. But on the outside, he or she struggles to look in control, presenting a calm facial expression, unhurried gestures, and relaxed speech. This dissonance between inner state and outer appearance interrupts the flow of the emotion—fear. If the individual permits the fear to flow, a healthy resolution is more likely.

Consider a client who came to me for help with his fear of public speaking. This was particularly onerous for him because his career required making plenty of speeches and public presentations. He would quake in terror before each speech, and then struggle throughout to look "just fine," concluding each episode in a state of emotional and physical exhaustion.

"Does the wind try not to blow?" I asked him.

"What? No. Of course not. It just blows," he replied.

"So, why don't you just shake and be nervous?" I challenged.

"Because I don't want to look stupid," he said.

"You're telling me that you're ashamed of being stupid."

"Yes. I guess I am."

"Well, the wind isn't ashamed of blowing, so why don't you just tell your audience that you're nervous?" I suggested.

"Tell the audience? You must be joking. I couldn't tell them that!" he replied.

"Why not?"

"They'd think I was . . . I was . . . ah . . ."

"You were what?" I pressed.

"Well . . . nervous," he concluded.

"Yes, they would. And I'll bet you dollars-to-donuts that 95 per cent of your audience gets nervous about public speaking, too," I suggested. "If you want to get over this, you need to quit blocking your anxiety and flow with it."

"Like the wind," he muttered.

"Yes. Let anxiety blow."

He selected a low-profile speaking engagement to field test my recommendation. He began his talk by telling the audience that, "I get nervous when I have to speak in front of groups, so bear with me if I look a little shaky at times."

Darn near every head in the place was nodding with understanding and empathy, and the speech went splendidly. As one might expect, his fear all but disappeared once he openly acknowledged it—once he quit interrupting the flow of his emotion and displayed harmony between what he felt, what he thought, and how he behaved. That's flow. It makes living much more natural; not always pleasant, but at least harmonious.

Many of us unconsciously recognize the need to create flow. Our attraction to music, both human-made and natural, reflects this response. We listen to songs that seem to reflect our inner states, that "feel" the way we feel. People often say, "This song says it for me."

The songs and flows of nature will connect with us in this manner, as well, and more profoundly, if only we pay attention. They are perhaps less easily discerned by those not accustomed to listening to nature, but they are deeply powerful.

Nature's melodies—created by the waters, wind, animals, sky, plants—sing in a cadence that we already know deep in our souls, but have often forgotten. Nature's music is the elemental sound, like the beating of our mother's heart while we still resided in her womb, but the Earth Mother's sound is even more fundamental. It lives in the pulsations of our cells and tissues, the bio-rhythms of our organic systems, the staccato of the synapses firing in our brains. It is a sound we know in a place beyond conscious knowing. It's a sound that is "out there" in nature but also "in here" within the confines of what we each call "me."

I send many clients who are suffering from inner discord into the natural world to seek out and merge with the Earth's flows and harmonies. Those who manage to physically blend themselves with a flow state in nature experience a kind of re-tuning, as if they were a guitar or piano. Psychologists long have known that physiological states create and maintain emotional states. For example, we know that when people deliberately furrow their brows, they actually begin to feel troubled or grumpy. As another instance, it is possible to create and sustain an emotional state of depression simply by eating poorly, not getting any exercise, and failing to get sufficient sleep. Physiology profoundly influences emotion.

Consequently, when people use their bodies to merge with natural processes that are in harmony, they begin to experience a similar harmony in their physical being and, consequently, in their emotions. If you don't buy that, just float around in a hot tub for awhile. It's the human substitute for natural hot springs. You'll experience how physiology creates psychology.

I suggested to a woman client who was in discord that she try walking and sitting in a tall grass prairie on windy days, allowing her arms, legs, head, and torso to "wave" like the native grasses and flowers surrounding her.

"I let the wind move me," she explained later. "When it blew hard, I would bow over further. When it slackened, I sprang back, just like the grass."

Eventually, she hummed in synchronization with her movements and the whooshing of the wind, producing a flow between her body and the natural processes in which she was immersed. The result?

"Harmony. I felt really together, fluid, and relaxed," she reported.

A burly factory worker who came to me full of bitterness and mental turmoil regained his sense of flow in a trout stream on his parents' ranch.

"I just slipped my butt into that cool water on a hot day, grabbed ahold of an overhanging branch to stay in place, and floated in the current. I let my body and legs just wave with the water," he told me.

"How did it make you feel?" I asked. Psychotherapists, ever predictable, ask this question more than any other.

"Great. My troubles just sort of floated away, if you know what I mean. Only bad thing was, I was hoping a big rainbow trout would swim into my trunks, but no cigar."

Other clients have tuned up their inner rhythms under waterfalls, on sand dunes, sailing, climbing trees, in snow drifts, canoeing, playing in the mud, fly fishing, or by simply watching a campfire. The more they were able to blend with the natural process they chose, the more they experienced rhythmic harmony between their emotions, thoughts, and actions.

Like the Pied Piper, the Earth's music draws us in. It leads us down nature's way. When we listen and watch and feel her flowing, then we remember, deeply, the rhythm that sustains order and structure in life.

We regain that order.

The natural order.

EXERCISE:

CEREMONY OF FLOW

Discord between one's emotions, thoughts, and actions is epidemic in our modern, Earth-alienated world. With regularity we are taught to hide our emotions, think and act differently than we feel, and be dishonest with both ourselves and others about what is actually occurring beneath our skins. In contrast, the realms of nature are resplendent with forthright rhythm and harmonic interplay between divergent forces and elements. While many of us fumble and stumble in our contrasts and psychological polarities, the Earth veritably dances. When we feel "out of synch," we can try to regain a sense of flow.

- Identify a location in nature where flow is both obvious and available, such as a beach, a waterfall, a wind-swept field or prairie, a river or stream, or a pine forest on a windy day. In particular, settings with water or wind are very conducive.
- If possible, physically "enter" the flow of the wind, water, sound, and so on. If not possible (say at a beach with heavy, dangerous surf), place yourself in close but safe proximity to the flowing process.
- Synchronize some aspect of your behavior with that of the flowing state in nature. This can include movement of your head, hands, or entire body, use of your voice (as in chanting), or both in tandem.
- A useful substitute is to employ audio or videotapes. There are many of these available which capture flow sights and sounds from nature—waterfalls, babbling brooks, wind, bird calls, crickets, and so on.
- The critical element, whether actually in a natural setting or simply listening to one on audiotape, is to move and vocalize in harmony with the Earth's flow. For most people, it is not as powerful and helpful to sit passively and observe or listen.

Example: A fifty-something woman who came for my assistance during her difficult divorce was in dire need of a sense of flow. While wracked with fear, anger, and sorrow on the inside, she felt compelled to maintain an outer countenance of relative calm and maturity. Even around close friends and family, she found it all but impossible to let her painful feelings flow, to release them. At my suggestion, she went to a pine forest in an isolated park on a blustery day. She attempted to harmonize her humming voice with the surfing sound of the high winds in the trees. While this proved awkward at first, eventually she was able to loosen her inhibitions sufficiently to dissolve her emotional armor. Her humming grew into howling, then sobbing. The sounds of the wind in the trees directed her vocal intensities like a maestro does an orchestra.

In this ceremony we enter Earth's flow and absorb it into our own being. We follow her lead in the dance of life.

CHANGING PLACES

Inside yourself or outside, you never have to change what you see, only the way you see it.

Author Thaddeus Golas

"I want to change."

If some other sentence has been spoken more often in psychotherapy, I don't know what it might be.

When we are disquieted or in outright turmoil, the cry for change comes straight from the heart. We humans do many hasty and sometimes foolish things in response to this inner clamor—drink too much, hop from job to job, relationship to relationship, town to town, buy stuff we don't need, say "yes" when we mean "no" and vice versa, work ourselves into a near-death experience, make resolutions or commitments we have little or no hope of keeping . . . well, you get the idea. You've probably also gotten the urges, and perhaps acted on them. If so, you're not alone.

A story may illustrate the point. One fine June afternoon, I was blessed to be crewing on a sailboat for a race on Lake Michigan. It was a long contest, and the fleet was spread out in an unusually orderly, compact line. The day was superb—about 12 knots of air, a cloudless sky, and temperatures in the high 70s. Great sailing weather. Our crew of seven was lulled a bit by these beneficent circumstances, so we didn't notice the black and white froth charging across the water at us from the windward shore until a hubbub arose from some nearby boats.

Headed our way was what is commonly called a "clear air squall." There are no clouds, rain, or thunder, just a sudden windstorm that announces its approach by churning the top of the water into a fuzzy frenzy called "spindrift." By the time we'd found our feet, this unwelcome visitor was but a couple hundred yards off our port beam and closing fast. It nailed us and the rest of the fleet about the time I'd pulled a couple wraps of the halyard off the cleat, hoping to get the sail down before the wind hit. No such luck.

A 60-knot wall of wind buffeted our forward sail like a fist smacking a paper wall, instantly exploding it into tattered pieces. We heeled over hard to starboard, as did all the other boats, until someone in the cockpit played out the mainsail far enough to ease the force of the blow. By then, the spindrift was blasting so hard across the deck that it was impossible to look anywhere but downwind, and in doing so, one merely saw a foggy morass of driving spray.

Basically, we just held on for dear life.

In the midst of this mayhem, our skipper bellowed at the crew member in charge of the mainsail.

"Do something!" he screamed over the howling maelstrom.

"What? What should I do?" the crewman hollered back.

"I don't know . . . just do something!"

That's how the impetus for change often arises in our psyches. We don't know what to do, but we sure feel the need to do something. Given this uncertainty, and knowing, as many of us do, that time can be quite an agent of change in and of itself, we sometimes elect to just wait and let matters resolve themselves. Which is largely what we did on the sailboat that wild and woolly day. In about five minutes the wind had eased to 45 knots, and within half an hour we were back to pre-gale serenity.

But being the action-oriented creatures we are, going with the flow of gradual transformation is not often our preference, and even if it is, there are many times in life when doing *something*, as opposed to nothing, is a good idea. But what should one do? A lot of folks walk in my door with that question on their lips.

"How do I make myself change?" many ask.

The notion of making changes is the crux of our dilemma. As with any living thing, human changes are better grown than made, at least in the personal and interpersonal arenas. Changing one's hairdo or the wallpaper in the bathroom is one thing, while changing one's vocation, emotional life, spiritual values, or outlook on living is quite another.

In general, Americans usually approach change the same way we approach the environment—we tear things up and put them back together the way we please. If we don't like how a river runs, we build dams and levees and try to compel nature to do our bidding, ignoring the wisdom that created something that works well if left alone. Similarly, people who don't like how they feel, think, or behave often grab their psyches by the throat and try to throttle them into submission. Sometimes a little throttling is necessary to get started, particularly if one is struggling to turn away from a chemical or behavioral addiction to alcohol, other drugs, food, or gambling. But most often, heavy-handed approaches to change work, if at all, for only a short time; generally until an emotional or situational flood surges forth to breach our newly constructed "dams and levees."

Personal transformation is best cultivated by partnering with the supreme agent of change, the Earth. Life is change, and nature is the wizard who enlivens its magic cycles. Each of us has, at most, a few decades of experience with the process of personal change, so even when we augment our brief background with the counsel of experts and sages, it hardly compares with the Earth's four-billion-year resumé in the field. Altering an individual organism's existence is no great shakes next to creating whole species, hoisting mountains from the plains, melting glaciers, or raising islands out of the sea bed. Still, in our hubris, we have overlooked the Earth's immense proclivity for change. Instead, we have done our best to modify many of her achievements by tinkering with or destroying entire ecosystems, rivers, forests, lakes, and other magnificent natural wonders.

Each of us is a product of nature as well, and like the Army Corps of Engineers setting itself upon the Mississippi, we can do far more damage by muscling our way through personal changes than by harmonizing our efforts with natural rhythms.

Change-by-demand is an arrogant attitude, and one that many of us apply to our own psychological ecosystems, as well as the larger biosphere. When we don't like how we feel, think, or behave, we whistle in the mental bulldozers and have at it; have at *us*, that is. But like the forces of life on the Earth, the forces in our personalities rarely surrender outright to our landscaping efforts. Often, they unravel the artificial changes we impose upon ourselves, and each "new me" turns back into "the old me" in short order.

Many of us have experienced this process. We cram some change down our psyche's throat by, as examples, adopting an artificial optimism to disguise our customary pessimism, feigning assertiveness to overlay our timidity, pledging a New Year's resolution to eat better, exercise, or stop smoking, or making a commitment to be a more loving spouse despite the fact that we're not in love at all. The list of shotgun transformations is endless. When imposed with sufficient force, any given change may stay in place awhile, but usually it figures a way to slip out the back door when your conscious mind isn't looking.

Gary's conundrum illustrated this impasse. He came to me because he suffered from anxiety attacks—intense surges of fear and apprehension that convinced him he was going crazy, dying, or both. Over a two-year span, Gary force-fed himself all the recommended methods for disposing of his attacks—relaxation training, systematic desensitization, tranquilizers, cognitive therapy (using your thoughts to master your emotions), and biofeedback. All to no avail. The adrenaline surges kept returning.

"How can I get rid of this damn panic?" he asked me.

"You can't," I replied.

"Then what's the use?"

"Wait. I said *you* can't. Obviously, you've tried, and you have proven beyond any reasonable doubt that *you* can't get rid of your anxiety."

"So who can . . . you?" he asked with healthy skepticism.

I shook my head.

"Wait a minute. Is this some religious pitch? Are you gonna tell me that if I just give myself over to God, that my anxiety will disappear, that I'll experience a miracle or something?"

That earned another negative nod.

I wasn't teasing the man. I was attempting to point him away from the avenues he had already pursued unsuccessfully—specifically, trying to force himself to change, and relying on some expert to change him.

"Tell me something besides an anxiety attack that would really scare you," I said.

"Lots of things. I mean, being in a jet that was going down, or getting attacked on the street, or falling off a cliff, or . . . "

"How about something that would really scare you but not kill you at the same time?" I asked.

"Being alone and lost in the woods at night. That would scare me," he replied.

"So, you really, really want to change, eh?" I asked.

"Oh, my god . . . not the woods at night." His eyes widened at the thought.

Anxiety is funny business. Gary's wasn't directly caused by the woods at night. In fact, as near we could figure, it had no cause at all. For most of us, anxiety isn't about real dangers, but rather about imagined ones, or those that are real but unconscious and nameless. A lot of folks who are wracked by anxiety attacks can't pinpoint what is frightening them, except perhaps the experience of fear itself. They just get very, very wired for no obvious reason.

Like all our emotions, fear is born in nature, as we are. Through contact with nature, we can experience fear or any of our primary feelings in a very fundamental and primitive way.

I began to recognize the Earth as the origin of our emotional lives years ago when I introduced the subject of werewolves, of all things, at a party. Maybe these hairy horrors came to my mind because we were sitting in the dark on a porch, and a full moon was rising over Little Bay de Noc at the top of Lake Michigan. In any case, I asked the assembled if they believed in these menacing creatures.

"Get real!" all the men and most of the women intoned, laughing me off.

"I do," one woman finally admitted, taking a lot of ribbing for doing so.

"Why?" I asked. "Why would a perfectly rational, adult woman believe in werewolves?"

"Because I've felt the fear in all of us. You know, that deep down fear that scares us into wondering if maybe there really are monsters." She tried to explain amidst the merciless chiding of the other guests.

This woman spoke of the stark terror that sometimes strikes at us from nature, such as being caught in a vicious storm or finding one's self lost and disoriented in the wild. In nature, as in all of us, there is the dark side, the shadow. The capricious mayhem of the tornado or hurricane, the vicious cunning of the predator set upon its prey, the blackness of night when we cannot see but can be seen, the poisonous viper or insect, the chaos of a raging forest fire—all present us with the menacing side of the life force.

"If you were alone in the middle of the forest tonight beneath that full moon, and you were lost and without a flashlight, don't you imagine that the thought of werewolves might cross your mind?" I asked the other guests.

All acknowledged that it might.

If actually in this situation, some of these folks would have dismissed the thought outright, others would have used reasoning to fight it off, and still others would have whistled in the dark, but all would have felt the cold breath of fear pass across their hearts. All our elemental fears reside in that moment of wondering what is real and what is not, and not being sure. This same elemental fear is what breaks the surface of our lives like a black gusher and manifests itself in many guises, such as panic attacks, fear of failure, of death, of rejection, and all the rest.

Hoping to bring him face-to-face with the ground floor of his fright, I persuaded Gary to wander off alone and get lost in the woods late one afternoon, equipped with a flashlight, tent, sleeping bag, warm clothing, food, and water. He agreed to stay out there until morning, and then find his way back somehow. I promised him that if he didn't phone me by noon, I would call the Mounties. I neglected to mention that the woods were outside of their jurisdiction.

It was a tough assignment for anyone who is not at home in the forest or in the dark, but even more so for a person like Gary, whose life was ruled by fear. But the cry to "Do something!" can be so powerful that we will sometimes do whatever is required to break free from the emotional traps that have ensnared us.

Gary spent his wide-eyed night on nature's dark side, in its shadow. Like Luke Skywalker of "Star Wars," he descended into the pit to face the basis of his fear—the terror of being alone, defenseless, and blind. As one might anticipate, it was an agonizing passage.

"I didn't sleep a wink. I didn't use the flashlight because I didn't want to be seen. I tried to be absolutely still, not make a sound, but I knew there were things out there that could see and smell me.

Sometimes I heard them nearby crunching the leaves or breaking a twig," he recounted, shaking a bit at the thought.

"What things?" I asked. "What were they?"

Gary thought about that question for some time before giving his answer.

"It doesn't matter what they actually were. The things that scared me were more in my imagination than they were out there in the dark," he replied. "And that's what I figured out. When I have these panic attacks, I'm scared by what I can't see, by what really isn't there. There's nothing there except the *possibility* of something, and I'm scared of what might be, not what is, if that makes any sense."

"It's one of the better descriptions of anxiety that I've heard, Gary. Are you glad you did it?" I asked.

"Nope. I'm glad it's over."

Gary's anxiety problem gradually evaporated, and he didn't *make* this change happen. He *grew* the change. He *grew* out of his anxiety. The embryo of that growing was planted in the crucible of his terror in a dark forest, alone, and like a flower seed delivered from the darkness, it sprouted and reached for the light.

Changes *made* by thinking things through, by arm-twisting behavior modification and other forced, direct methods, differ from those *grown* out of experience, emotional journeys, and ritual. One can rightfully argue that our approach to Gary's problem was loosely aimed. His anxiety attacks bore no obvious relationship to his fear of being in the dark woods, yet he changed in response to that experience.

When we seek change of a deep and fundamental sort, the most helpful course is often one of broad cultivation, not finely focused mental surgery. We need to place ourselves in a context where an experience of change becomes possible. By allowing change to occur through meaningful contact with the Earth, rather than forcing it to happen within our minds, bodies, or human relationships, we employ the same methodology as the farmer. We take our "seed" to the spiritual soil of the natural world, plant and cultivate it, and then trust in the life force to take us where we need to go. Gary planted the seeds of change in the soil of his fearful relationship with the Earth, a relationship based on dread, but also one fraught with the potential of transforming his way of experiencing himself in the world.

The natural world is replete with "change places," physical locations and life processes that afford us transformative energies and experiences. Native peoples in North America, as one example, actively utilized the Earth for promoting personal change and for furthering individual rites of passage. The Sun Dance of the Plains Indians, the vision quest and lamenting on the mountain or butte found in many Amerindian cultures, and the spiritual purification of the sweat lodge ceremony of the Lakota Sioux are but a few examples of this ancient psycho-spiritual tradition.

When I assist clients with personal change, we often proceed more or less along these steps:

- Clarify the emotions and behaviors that the person wants to change.
- Find an available location or life process in the natural world that bears some analogous relationship to those emotions and behaviors; a place or process that brings the person more acutely into awareness or alters habitual patterns.
- Determine a transforming action (ritual) that will afford the person a deep and meaningful experience of those emotions and behaviors, potentially revealing a new direction for that individual's relationship with those emotions and behaviors.

As another example, a woman sought my assistance with her timidity. She felt unable to assert herself in most social situations, and this interfered greatly with her effectiveness in her career and with satisfaction in her personal relationships. She had taken courses in assertiveness training, done some role playing with another counselor, and used visualization and mental affirmations in an effort to bolster her self-confidence, all to little avail. We addressed her desire for change by:

- Clarifying how she wanted to feel and act, which primarily included feeling more confident, valuing herself and her contributions more, and actively interjecting her ideas, opinions, and emotions into her relationships with people.
- Finding a challenging location and process in nature, which consisted of some river rapids in a nearby state forest.
- Determining how she would interact assertively with this natural process (the rapids), which involved (1) wading into the river, (2) walking upstream against the onrushing current, and (3) speaking her opinions and feelings loudly enough to be heard over the roar of the water.

There is an obvious distinction between this kind of change process and those promoted in traditional psychotherapy. Growing changes by interacting with the natural world is an artistic and metaphorical process rather than a technical and literal one. It invokes imagination, symbolic action, the "writing" of one's own ritualistic story of transformation, and, often, a degree of surrendering control rather than seizing it.

There is great transformative power and spiritual energy in our Earth Mother's domain and within her life forces. When a person blends the impetus for change ("Do something!") with the ever-present evolutions and cycles of the natural world, then she or he will be transformed, sometimes in ways never anticipated. In interacting with the life force, one cannot dictate the exact course of one's changes anymore than one can control the direction of the wind.

Change is not always about taking control.

Often, it is about letting go, about trusting one's deeper self to dance harmoniously with the life force, with the Earth.

It's about trust between child and Mother.

Chapter Eleven

Blending

*Grown men may learn from very little children,
for the hearts of little children are pure and,
therefore, the Great Spirit may show to them
many things which older people miss.*

Lakota Medicine Man Black Elk

"Hug a tree," was an adage that became popular during the first Earth Day more than two decades past. As an activity, it was already prevalent among hippies during the 60s, who engaged in tree-hugging while in varying states of drug-induced reverie.

Hugging trees is fine, but there's more to blending with nature than that.

"I want you to be like a tree," I told Mike, a 20-something client.

"Be like a tree?" His face crumpled in disbelief. "How am I supposed to be like a tree, and why the hell would I want to?"

"Have you ever been like a tree before?" I asked.

"Of course not. I'm a person. I don't go around playing like I'm a fricking tree!"

After years of suggesting such things to people, I've grown accustomed to incredulous reactions. Frankly, given my own cultural background, I probably would have reacted similarly when I was in my 20s. Mike's is a culturally mediated skepticism. Our customary, "You must be kidding!" recoil to such ideas is further evidence of how far most of us have drifted from our Mother.

"When you were a kid, did you ever make believe you were an animal, like a lion or something?" I asked.

"Sure. And monkeys, wolves, lots of animals," Mike replied.

"So, if I asked you to be like a wolf, you probably could pull that off, provided you didn't feel too embarrassed?"

"I suppose. I wouldn't do it in public or anything, but I could walk around on all fours and howl like a wolf if I wanted to . . . which I don't," he added quickly.

"Fine. So what's the big deal about pretending to be a tree?"

"I could do it, I guess, but what the hell for?" he demanded.

Tactfully, and with considerable reframing, I went on to explain how some trees possess the qualities (personality) he told me he wanted but lacked: perseverance, strength, and steadfastness. Mike described himself as wishy-washy, weak, and easily discouraged. His personal characteristics were almost the direct opposite of the qualities found in certain trees—oak, elm, hickory, and ironwood, for example.

"I think a stout tree may have something to teach you, but you'll have to approach it like a kid. You'll have to make-believe," I explained.

"How the hell is a tree going to teach me anything?" he demanded.

There it was again, that reflexive human penchant to place ourselves above nature, as if we have nothing to learn from it, nothing to gain by experiencing its reality as distinct from our own. Human arrogance.

"If you're willing to blend with it, a tree can help you feel the qualities you've told me you want," I replied. "You aren't going to acquire these qualities by talking to me or reading some self-help book, but you may be able to learn about them from a tree. That is, if you let yourself."

"I'm supposed to learn how to be a better person from a tree? Just how am I going to do that?" he asked, incredulously.

It took me awhile to convince Mike to set aside his oh-so-adult pride, open his oh-so-shut mind, and give nature a chance. It usually takes awhile. The idea that the Earth, through her many living forms, has the capacity to communicate wisdom to us is abjectly foreign to most modern folks. It just isn't part of our belief system, although it has been a hallmark of many indigenous cultures far into the distant past. The false pride that permeates most of us, the pride that suggests we are above nature, stands between us and the humility that is a prerequisite to learning from nature.

Nobody who thinks he or she knows it all will ever learn much of anything, and such an attitude is all too common in how people regard the natural world. But we don't know it all, as anyone who has wrestled with a vexing personal problem can attest. In fact, in the realm of emotions, mental states, and spirituality, we don't know much.

Eventually, I managed to convince Mike to "make like a tree," but it wasn't as easy as falling off a log. The prescribed exercise was simple. He was told to walk about in a woods of his choice until he came upon a tree that seemed to embody the characteristics he desired. We often tell people who want to learn something to pick out a mentor, a role model, a hero, or someone who manifests the attributes they wish to emulate, and to learn from that individual. Why not learn from some other living entity or process? People are not the only good role models. Some would argue that, on the whole, people are less trustworthy role models than many animals and plants.

Anyway, Mike was counseled to find a tree that "grabbed him" in a certain way, just as some jewelry or an article of clothing grabs the shopper who is searching for that just right gift. What seized his imagination was a relatively young black walnut, one that was perhaps 30 feet tall.

His next task was to "get acquainted" with the tree. This involved studying it with his eyes, first close up, then from some distance, and at various angles. Next, he used his hands to feel the bark and stroke the leaves, and to inspect the base. Finally, he smelled the tree. I could not persuade him to taste it.

Once familiarity was established, he was instructed to assume a posture that approximated the general look of the tree. This is a bit tricky for the literal-minded, but just as a child can pretend to be a bird, a shark, or a snake, to which she or he bears little resemblance, so an adult can figuratively reflect almost any creature or thing. Given the proper social context, we are comfortable with impersonating people, but feel weird about impersonating trees and the like. In the relative safety of playing a game, like pantomime, adults can be persuaded to make-believe, but most consider therapy serious business.

In reality, play is one of the more effective forms of therapy.

Finally, Mike was instructed to "do" what the tree was doing. In this case he stood straight and stalwart but also moved as the branches did to the touch of the wind. He stood this way for a time, feeling the breeze blow through his "branches," imaginatively experiencing himself rooted deeply into the soil and absorbing the hot energy of the sun as if photosynthesis were occurring within his own cells. This sort of make-believe "doing" usually leads to "feeling like," as it did for Mike despite his initial skepticism.

In those brief and at first silly moments, Mike was surprised to find himself feeling the qualities of the tree—youthful strength, determination to grow, harmony with the surroundings, quiet patience, and consistency. Buoyed by this new experience, he positioned himself with his back against the tree, closed his eyes and felt himself joining with it.

"You'll think this is weird, but for a moment I almost felt like I was drawing strength from that tree," he reported.

"Doesn't sound the least bit weird to me," I reassured him. "We draw strength from the air we breathe, from the Earth's foods, from the water we drink, and from sunlight. Why not from a tree?"

As any physicist can tell us, all matter is actually energy encapsulated in a physical form. Analogously, emotions are energy in motion. People, trees, rocks, water, feelings, clouds . . . all are different expressions of the basic energy that comprises the Earth. Each of these may look and feel very different to us, but at the sub-atomic level (the building block level), each is essentially the same. Trees and people may look like distinct, solid objects, but at the quantum level, they are more similar than different. This fundamental similarity makes the idea of trees and people "communicating" far less outrageous.

When Mike established contact with the walnut tree, he was, at the basic level of physics, bringing his life energies into close association with those of the tree. He was seeking to blend his life force with that of another living entity. People experience this blending most clearly during truly intimate lovemaking, when each lover's sense of being a separate person slips away and two become as one. While trees and people do not make love, they can make contact.

Blending with natural elements and forces can involve an almost infinite array of venues. I have worked with clients who accomplished blending with mountains, rivers, boulders, animals (both wild and domesticated), fog, sand, surf, trees and other flora, prairies, deserts, gardens (both natural and human-cultivated), waterfalls, caves, snow-drifts . . . even mud. Many, though not all, found that these encounters touched them in some vital place, precipitating emotional and spiritual changes.

Those who did benefit from blending frequently questioned me about the "true nature" of their experiences.

"Was this just a placebo effect?" several asked. "You know, if you think it will help, then it does?"

"Did I just make this up in my imagination, or do I really feel different?" a few have inquired.

"Do you really believe that a mountain (as one example) has some sort of spiritual energy or something that people can draw from?" others have asked.

My basic response to these wonderings has been little or no response, not because I'm secretive, but because rediscovering one's bond with the Earth is an experiential event, not one composed of religious or intellectual dogma. It's not that I'd rather avoid interpreting the meaning of these events. I truly don't *know* what they mean. I do, however, have some sense of what these dances with nature accomplish, so I encourage people to make contact and feel the healing and sustaining qualities of the Earth. However they choose to pin the intellectual tail on this donkey is their business, not my own.

Like any approach to healing, blending is not for everyone, although it probably could be if more minds and hearts were open to it. It seems most helpful for (1) those who have the capacity and willingness to access the part of themselves that remains a playful child, and (2) those who already believe that the Earth is a living essence with profound emotional and spiritual energies. Even those who do not embrace the notion of Earth-as-Mother can positively participate in blending, provided they can temporarily suspend judgment and openly embrace the inherent possibilities.

Not everyone can. Some of us find the idea of the Earth as a living, interacting entity with its own consciousness, emotional characteristics, and healing qualities so foreign that we refuse to test our preconceptions in the laboratory of personal experience. Show me a closed mind, and I'll show you a pretense of an "expert," someone who presumes to know answers before legitimately asking and experimenting with the questions. As the adage goes, "In the beginner's mind there are many possibilities, while in the expert's mind there are few."

Like the Earth, like the life force itself, living is about possibilities. When we stop entertaining them, we stop living.

Blending with nature invokes new possibilities: those that can be grown from the human spirit and those that can be reaped from the emotional and spiritual essences of animals, plants, elements, and natural forces. It is a way of joining with our Mother, of drawing from her what she gave us to begin with.

Life.

EXERCISE:

CEREMONY OF BLENDING

All of us are mentally and emotionally absorbent to some degree. We assimilate emotional states, attitudes, ways of perceiving reality, and behaviors from other people and situations. These assimilation experiences can be as conscious as a child's decision to "be like" her or his hero, and as unconscious as a spouse's reflexive tendency to adopt the emotional tone of his or her partner (commonly called "co-dependency"). In kind, we can deliberately absorb qualities and attributes of the natural world.

- Determine the characteristic you wish to assimilate. These may vary from a specific emotional state, such as joy or love, to a personality attribute, such as forthrightness or courage, to a certain behavior, like assertiveness or silence.
- Seek a natural entity, process, or place that appears to embody the characteristic you have identified.
- To the degree physically possible, blend with that natural aspect. Assume its characteristics and behaviors. Mirror and "be like" the wind, a tree, the waves, an open field, a mountain, a cloud, or a field of wild flowers, to name a few.
- As you immerse yourself in this blending process, do your best to set aside thinking, analysis, and self-consciousness. *Be* that part of nature. If you have difficulty in this regard, practice a brief breathing meditation or relaxation technique before initiating blending.
- Blending can be facilitated or enhanced through sensory absorption. Employ all your senses—touching, seeing, hearing, smelling—in an effort to drink in the aspects of nature that you wish to absorb.
- Continue blending until you feel some change in your mood, mental state, or behavior which indicates that you have absorbed the characteristic of that natural process, object, or place. At times, the change may not be what you expected. Some of my clients have blended with a particular part of nature, expecting to absorb a certain

attribute, only to discover they had assimilated something entirely different. We can't always predict the innate characteristics of natural elements and processes until we experience them directly.

- Take a moment to express your gratitude to Mother Earth for her assistance. Some of my clients feel the urge to thank the specific entity or process in nature with which they blended. Whatever your comfort level in this regard, I encourage you to at least make a silent expression of thankfulness.

Example: A woman sought my assistance in using "mind over matter" to become pregnant. Medical tests had failed to demonstrate any physical impediment to her and her husband conceiving a child, yet several frustrating years had gone by without their being successful in doing so. The obvious characteristic she sought was fertility, an aspect of nature that is intense and widespread. Rich, midwestern soil became the object of her blending efforts. She spent time almost every day lying face-down on the soil, trying to soak in its life-giving characteristics. In three months she was pregnant. Cause and effect or merely coincidence? I left that question for her to answer. "I will always feel a special bond with the soil," she later told me. That was all the answer she needed.

TOUCHING THE EARTH

The old people came literally to love the soil and they sat or reclined on the ground with a feeling of being close to a mothering power. The soil was soothing, strengthening, cleansing and healing. That is why the old Indian still sits upon the earth instead of propping himself up and away from its life-giving forces. For him, to sit or lie upon the ground is to be able to think more deeply and to feel more keenly; he can see more clearly into the mysteries of life and come closer in kinship to other lives about him . . .

Lakota Chief Luther Standing Bear

Jean had suffered many losses.
In the space of a couple years, her husband died suddenly of a heart attack, her father suffered a debilitating stroke, her daughter ran off to Europe to be with a going-nowhere-fast boyfriend, her best friend moved across the country, and she lost her job due to a corporate downsizing. By the time she shuffled into my office, she'd lost 20 pounds off her already slim frame, developed an unhappy cornucopia of psychosomatic symptoms, and had become an expert on how to get by with three hours of sleep a night.
There was no glib panacea for Jean's long string of misfortune. She could talk, cry, and scream, and get some cathartic relief in the process, but the emotional and spiritual disequilibrium caused by so much loss and tragedy could not be dissolved by mere talk.
"With such people, all you can do is listen and let time do its best,"

I was once advised. But Jean needed more than an ear and a calendar.

"You ever do any gardening?" I asked toward the end of our second counseling session.

"Not lately, but when I was a kid, I raised flowers, tomatoes, carrots, and other stuff," she replied in a detached monotone, staring off into the dark spaces of her overburdened psyche.

"It's time to be a kid again," I counseled. "You need a garden."

Although she couldn't see the sense in it, Jean passively complied with my oddball suggestion. As I recommended, she had a handyman come and till a garden space in her backyard, even though it was July. Then she returned to me for further instructions.

"Okay. The garden space is ready. Now what?" she asked at our next visit.

"Now, it's time to get dirty," I replied. "I want you to dig around in the dirt. No gloves. Just get your hands into that soil. Be sure to get plenty of it under your fingernails, too."

"Sounds pretty weird. Don't you want me to plant something?"

"Later. For now, just get your fingers in the muck."

So Jean did. She felt a tad strange about it at first, crawling around on her hands and knees in a garden of dirt with no bulbs, no hand spade, no seeds, just good old black earth. But her embarrassment passed quickly. She sat in the soil, lifted it in her cupped hands like water, squeezed it between her fingers, dug, and then evened it out. Basically, she played in the mud.

"It felt good," she later told me. "There's something about the feel of the earth. I can't describe it other than to say that it felt real and alive. It was comforting."

My mother, who comes from generations of Irish farmers, always took her worries and woes to her garden.

"Just getting your hands into the soil is healing," my mother told me. "It's like touching life."

Indeed it is.

Gardening is one of the finest psychotherapies that was never intended to be one. As Thomas Berry, an author of nature books, so aptly reminds us, "Gardening is an active participation in the deepest mysteries of the universe." Soil is the sustaining medium for many living things—bacteria (most of which are benign), food plants, flowers, prairie grasses, mosses, mushrooms, trees, all land animals (including humans), and countless other flora and fauna. When we get our hands and bodies into the dirt, we are co-mingling with the very stuff of which we are made, and by which we are sustained. We are, in a very real and tangible sense, returning to our source. Going home.

"When I touch the Earth, I feel solid, rooted," another client concluded.

Immersion in nature's substances is a powerful tonic for emotional dis-ease. Simple acts like digging our hands in the dirt, getting soaked in a rainstorm, rolling in a snow drift, taking a swim, sitting on the grass, or climbing a tree allow us to touch the Earth and feel her ageless, vibrant forces—the forces of life.

I advise many of my clients who are ungrounded and off balance due to grief, fear, sadness, obsessive worry, anger, or guilt to re-establish physical contact with the Earth.

While it is difficult, perhaps even impossible to describe in words, contact with the Earth's soil, water, and wind has pronounced effects on the mind and body (which are, despite our cultural distinctions, one and the same). In nature's touch there is both emotional comfort and a profound remembrance of who we are. In a literal and figurative sense, we become grounded.

To be sure, rubbing dirt on your hands won't wipe away your worries or resolve the all-too-real troubles that accompany every life, but it can bring back a sense of belonging, of solidity, and of hope. Such feelings make all problems easier to bear and often less exhausting to resolve.

As for Jean, we didn't stop with getting her hands dirty.

Soil, in particular, is a medium that manifests the circle of life and death, followed by new life. It is made from the decaying matter of countless living entities, some recent and others ancient, yet it is the life-sustaining substance that nurtures new plants and creatures. Simple dirt is a visible and miraculous manifestation of life's power to carry on. In addition to its practical value, the soil has tremendous spiritual significance, by not merely *symbolizing* the process of birth, growth, death, decay, and new birth, but by actually playing a vital role in that process.

People like Jean who are burdened with grief, can use the soil to help them cycle through to new life and new beginnings. They can accomplish this through ritual, by using spiritual substances (like the soil) to symbolically act out their losses and their hoped-for rebirths.

In Jean's case, I asked her to select some of her deceased husband's personal belongings that would readily degrade in the soil. This was a painful process for her, but she eventually decided upon an old love letter from their courtship, a scarf she'd made him for their first Christmas, and a wood carving he'd done for her on their 20th anniversary. Then I asked her to determine the best day and time for conducting a ritual with these items. She opted for a moonlit night, late, when she could have her privacy. Together, she and I worked out the form and sequence of the ritual itself, and then she waited for the proper night to present itself.

When a night felt right, she took these very personal items and went out to her unplanted garden. Using a small spade and her bare hands, she dug small "graves" for each of the articles, and then buried the personal symbols of her loss. Deep within her psyche and soul, she was giving her grief to the Earth, offering it as a kind of spiritual sacrifice in the hope that it might contribute to some rebirth in herself.

"The memories and tears just flowed," she told me later. "But for the first time, I really didn't feel alone in my grief. It seemed to be a part of something much greater, more meaningful. It's hard to describe, but that's what it was like."

With the symbols of her dead husband immersed in the soil, Jean planted bulbs for perennials on top of the small "graves."

"It's not enough that we grieve when someone or something dies in our lives. We have to grow new life out of death," she explained.

And that process—new life from death—is what soil is all about. When Jean carried out her ritual in the garden, she was doing more than performing a rite of passage. She was intimately interacting with the great circle of life, death, and renewal, not just in some symbolic sense, but literally by placing her own body in direct contact with the biological source from which she sprang and to which her husband had already returned. By completing the cycle of life and death, she was following nature's way of emotional healing.

She was home.

A few weeks later, Jean let go of much of her remaining grief during a heavy rain. She went out into the garden, knelt in the wet soil where she had planted the flowers and, with the downpour drenching her in a steady torrent, sobbed out the last of her deep mourning. Her tears of sadness and dying mingled with the Earth's own crying: the rain.

"The rain was the key," she told me. "In it I felt the tears of the Earth, like some great outpouring of sadness for all the creatures that have died since life began."

"Yet in that rain is new life," I reminded her. "The water and the soil and the seeds are all necessary to create rebirth."

"Yes," she agreed. "From that sad rain comes new life."

As is true of all of the Earth's wondrous processes, rain is not merely water falling out of the sky. It is not some inert substance involved in a mindless, mechanical process. Nor is it merely a symbol of life. It *is* life. So are the wind, the soil, clouds, rocks, rivers, and seas.

Through nature we experience the comfort that death is not the end, that we are intricately interwoven with the ageless transformation of life, and that dying, like being born, is a beginning. These words are just words until we feel the soil, the wind, the rain, and the snow upon our skin. Then we know in our hearts and hands as well as our minds that new life will come from death.

All this from just getting your fingernails dirty or just getting your body drenched? Yes, all this. Ask any person who works lovingly with the land. They will tell you that they absorb this comfort from the Earth. It may not jump out at them like profound scripture or the blinding light of revelation, but they feel it deep within themselves, like the moist warmth from holding a baby, like the feel of life as it billows up fresh in a stalk of corn, like the watery strength of the surf breaking on the beach, like the pungent smell of new-mown hay, or like the sun warming your face on a winter's day.

Touch the Earth.

She is alive.

E X E R C I S E :

CEREMONY OF PASSING

Loss and death sink the human spirit into sadness and mourning. Short of death itself, life is riddled with transitions that constitute little deaths. These losses of lesser or greater importance challenge us to transform our inner lives.

When we are depressed, even for no apparent reason, it is usually in response to some loss, consciously recognized or not. Perhaps life has wrested from us a love, a friend, a vocation, our health, a dream, or some other obvious asset. Or perhaps our loss is uncertain, primarily felt rather than intellectually ascertained. At such times, we can turn to the Earth to help us walk the path of dark change, the way of shadows.

- Create or identify some tangible thing that symbolizes or represents either what you have lost (if you know what that is) or the feeling of loss itself, the sadness, grief, and anger. This could be a gift from a deceased loved one or from a lover or spouse lost through rejection or divorce, as examples. If you are uncertain what material thing to use, you can write a letter about how you feel and what has happened to you, and use that as the object. Whatever it may be, this symbolic thing needs to be an object you are willing to part with.
- Next, determine a transformational process, a way of changing your symbolic object that has a life-to-death quality. Optimally, the transformational process you choose should feel intuitively similar to the emotional tone of your inner experience. For example, sadness which is deep, dark, and somber may be ceremonialized best through burial. In contrast, sadness which is singed with anger may transform most readily with burning. A strong sense of rejection or abandonment is sometimes best represented by leaving the symbolic object—a kind of metaphorical desertion.
- Select a natural context and a time to perform your ceremony. As with choosing a transformational process, selecting a setting should be guided by your inner emotional state. Preferably, the setting should be in a natural

place that conveys a spiritual ambiance for you, and should be suitable to the type of ceremony you wish to conduct. Some people find that the darkness and quiet of night reflects their feelings better than the day. Others wait for wind, rain, or snow, as any of these may provide an external atmosphere which reflects one's internal emotional atmosphere.

- Go to the location at the time and in the conditions you feel best reflect your inner state. Once there, spend a few moments meditating on the symbolic object and the feelings which it represents for you. Then conduct your ceremony, taking the object and transforming it in the manner you determined. Finally, meditate at the conclusion of the transformation, soliciting the Earth's healing spirit as an aid to your own emotional healing.

Example: A man in his 20s came to me for assistance with his intense grief over his former fiancé's sudden decision to break off their engagement and end the relationship. Despite many conversations with family and friends, he was unable to work through his distress. We decided to use a ceremony of passing. For his symbolic object, he selected a gift from his former fiancé—a gold chain. Although an expensive item, its use suited him because it deeply represented their former bond. For a setting, he decided upon a waterfall in a park where he had proposed marriage to her. For a time, he chose midday—the time of his proposal. His original intention had been to throw the chain into the deep pool at the base of the falls, but upon arriving there another intuitive impulse persuaded him otherwise. He waded into the water, held the chain up against the flow of the falls, and then let it go. This "letting go" transformational process was both literal (releasing the chain itself) and figurative (discharging his emotional bond to her, and so his sadness over its loss). The transformational aspect of the setting (moving water) further enhanced the spiritual significance of the ceremony, and its profound emotional impact upon him.

"Life is a series of losses," a colleague of mine maintains. By joining with our Earth Mother's tremendous powers of change, with her cycles of life and death, we can work through these difficult times, and not feel alone in them.

GROWING DECISIONS

Nature is man's teacher. She unfolds her treasures to his search, unseals his eye, illumes his mind, and purifies his heart; an influence breathes from all the sights and sounds of her existence.

Poet Alfred Billings Street

John grunted as he cleared the last few steps to the summit. Once there, he turned to survey the winding path that had guided him on his mile-long climb up the massive, iron-laden rock that the locals called "the hill." But it was, from a geological perspective, a rock of iron ore—a big one, to be sure, but a single rock nonetheless.

From his hard-won perch, John could see the pine and poplar strewn Lake Superior shore arching off in both directions, and he could hear the distant splash of waves on the rugged beach far below. But he hadn't made the climb for sightseeing. For the better part of a year, John had been writhing on the horns of a dilemma—his marriage. Uncertain of his wife's affections, particularly after she had a short but torrid affair, but also bedeviled by self-doubt about which course he should pursue, he had waited for fate to show him a sign. As so often occurs when we rely on fate, none had appeared.

"I can't decide whether to stay or go," he had confessed repeatedly during therapy sessions.

"You've made that quite clear," I replied just as often.

85

"So, how can I make this decision?" he asked.

"Not by thinking it over. You've been doing that for months," I suggested.

John's is a common approach to decision-making—thinking it over. And while some choices submit to rational analysis, those of the heart rarely cooperate. The heart has a will of its own, and that will is not subservient to rationalization or logic.

Like most who are perched atop an existential picket fence, John had sought counsel from many sources. He spoke with friends, with his minister, family members, and then myself. He read books and articles, watched television programs, and listened to radio talk shows, and he repeatedly endured the internal dialogue that accompanies circular thinking, in which "she loves me, she loves me not" never runs out of petals.

From none of these places did he secure an answer.

"This is not the kind of decision you can *make*. You need to go home and *grow* a decision," I suggested.

"What good will going home do? I live at home," he questioned.

"If only that were true, John," I replied. "I'm not speaking of the place with four walls where you take showers and eat corn flakes. I mean your heart's home."

It took awhile to convince John, as it does many, but eventually I persuaded him to seek the counsel of his Earth Mother, the only source he had left untapped. He was instructed to climb the hill early in the morning, taking along water, food, and rain gear, and then to stay at the summit "until the decision comes to you."

"What if I don't decide? Am I suppose to stay up there all night or what?" he asked.

"Stay until the decision comes," I repeated.

My words echoed in John's synapses as he settled on a smooth, rounded boulder that afforded a panoramic view of the shore well below. A lot of other words echoed in his head as well. He spent most of the morning and early afternoon replaying all the mentally taped conversations and suggestions that he had hoped would show him which way to go and hadn't. It was exhausting, maddening. Eventually, the voices of friends, counselors, and authors mingled with his own tortured thinking, forming a glob of mental mish-mash that, like bread dough, could never be separated into its constituent elements.

Finally, as evening approached, he tired of thinking it over.

Finding some mossy ground, he reclined for a short nap. The wind's whispers in the pines lulled him into a pleasant sleep, and he dreamed of nothing in particular. Upon waking, John found the sun close to the horizon and noticed the wind had pivoted more to the south, feeding warmer air up the hill on an offshore breeze. The growing pastels in the high cirrus clouds caught his eye, and hunger grabbed his gut. He ate and drank some juice, continuing to orient himself to the natural surroundings, and noticing things he'd missed entirely during his hours of obsessive rumination and mental replay. He realized that his thoughts had become quiet, as if they had never roused with him from the nap.

That felt good.

Soon the sun put down, painting a show of color and splash. John became fascinated with the gradual shift from day to night, particularly as it affected the sky and the shadows and hues cast upon the trees. He waited with child-like anticipation for the first star to punch through the blue sky that was shifting to black, and then watched the darkness fill in. As the stars appeared, it seemed as if some unseen hand were switching on tiny lights on the surface of some huge, distant sphere enclosing the Earth. He focused on one part of the sky, waiting for that first instant when a star would become visible so he could watch something emerging out of nothing. Little did he realize, but in the far recesses of his heart, something else was emerging out of nothing.

And so it went for hours into the darkness. He was sky gazing, not thinking, lying on his back, enfolded by the night—until he remembered his dilemma.

"It was so strange," he later told me. "I hadn't thought about it for hours, and then, suddenly I remembered that I had gone there to make a decision."

"And did you?" I asked.

"That's what was so odd," he reported, still a bit mystified. "The decision had already been made, I guess, while I wasn't thinking. Maybe it was like you said . . . it just grew while I wasn't watching."

"How?"

"I wish I knew for sure. Maybe it was the change in perspective, being outside and away from all the stuff that constantly reminded me of my problem. Maybe it was seeing those stars and realizing how much more there is to life than me and my problems. I'm just not sure," he said.

But he was sure of what was right for him.

"I realized that I was already emotionally divorced from my wife, and that what I was doing with all this indecision was stalling on the legal divorce. I knew that wasn't fair to her or to me," he said.

So, John took a final gaze at those stars, feeling them as friends and partners on some psychological quest, and then pulled out his flashlight and started down the hill.

"That place will always be special to me," he said.

"Sacred," I added.

"I guess so. I felt more peace and understanding there than I ever have in a church or a counselor's office. No offense. And I feel like I can go back there if I need to, if I get confused about something else or feel lost again," he added.

"You can," I assured him.

It wasn't important that John get some sermon from me about his need to bond with the Earth, or how immersion in the flow of nature can turn confused, troubled emotional waters into a certain, steady stream. He didn't need an intellectual interpretation of how the ever-growing power of the life force can help nurture a decision. I spared him my philosophical interpretations. After all, it was thinking that got him disjointed in the first place.

What he had learned on the summit was now set deep in his heart. He'd learned about going home, about finding one's spiritual bearings, about *growing* a decision rather than *making* one. And that learning was grounded in his experience, not in conceptual abstractions.

Our Earth Mother offers sound advice. It isn't wordy, glib, or crammed with psycho babble. In fact, it isn't even thoughtful.

It's heartful.

In the comfort of our Mother's fold, we can sometimes hear the truth in our own hearts, the truth we already know at some deep level of understanding, but which is buried under thick layers of cognitive sediment, thoughts upon thoughts upon thoughts.

When we return to our natural world, when its touches, songs, and visions transport us from our circuitous minds to our heartfelt senses, then we discover that spiritual place where decisions are grown, like all living things—raised up from the soil of emotion, intuition, and sensation.

Decisions, like living organisms, are not made. They are cultivated.

When we go out into the natural world and bring with us a choice that must be made, we plant the seed of that decision in the "soil" of the Earth's rhythms, moods, whispers, and wisdom, and allow it to sprout and grow. This "soil" is far different from the dry, shallow, and often rocky ground of the thinking mind. To be certain, thoughts have their place in decisions, particularly those that are pragmatic—which brand to buy, how to invest one's assets, or what route to travel. But in matters of the heart, involving relationships or life-making or breaking choices, the cognitive mind alone is clearly ill-equipped for the task.

When a choice looms before us, we will do well to spend as much or more time consulting the Earth than listening to all the inner and outer voices that claim to know what is best. Learning to trust her natural process frees us from thinking decisions to death. It is through nature that we recapture our sense of where we belong and which way to go. It is from such a steadfast and certain stance that important determinations should be grown.

The Earth is good at growing.

Even decisions grow in her care.

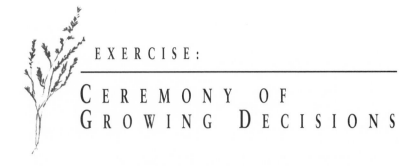

EXERCISE:

CEREMONY OF GROWING DECISIONS

Some decisions submit to rational analysis and judgment. Many do not. It's difficult to be deliberate and analytical about deciding whether to remain married, what vocation to pursue, or how to deal with a moral or ethical quandary. While our Earth Mother rarely decides matters for us outright, she provides an environment that can draw out our intuition and common sense–the cultivators of good decisions. She offers the existential perspective so often absent in the mind of someone who is gagged by and bound to a vexing choice. A ceremony for growing decisions seeks to combine the vast wisdom of the Earth with the innate sagacity of the human organism.

- Begin by clearly outlining the options available to you. If you experience difficulty, seek the input of a good friend, confidant, or counselor.
- Some find it helpful to create a physical representation of the decision that needs to be made, or of the options available. I have had clients draw or paint abstract pictures of their decisions or potential choices. Some have written a letter to themselves describing their dilemma.
- Once the characteristics of your decision are clear, it is time to create a quest—a journey into nature in search of an answer.
    1. Select a day to conduct the quest. That day may have some personal significance for you—an anniversary of some important event in your life, a day of the week or month that feels "right" for you, or even a birthday.
    2. Allow plenty of time. Being rushed on a quest defeats the purpose of *growing* a decision.
    3. Determine a place in nature for your journey. In most instances, a location that is new for you is best, for it will embody discovery, changed perspective, and fresh possibilities. To the degree possible, this location should be away from other people—in

parks, nature centers, national forests, or private farms or acreages to which you have access.

- As you begin your quest, truly *bring* the decision with you, either by holding it clearly in your mind or by carrying its physical representation (e.g., letter, drawing, etc.) with you. Some of my clients have meditated on their decision at the beginning by sitting quietly and visualizing, while others have spoken the equivalent of a short prayer, invoking their higher power to assist them.
- During your actual journey into and through the natural setting, it is often helpful to stop periodically and tune your sensory awareness to the surroundings. Often, our Earth Mother reaches out for the petitioning mind, offering insights and ideas. Be open to these. Watch for them.
- At some point, stop your physical journey in a location that feels rich with nature's presence and the vitality of the life force. Recognizing such a place is not that difficult. In all likelihood, you will sense "the right place" when you arrive there.
- Once situated, it helps to alternate between meditating on your decision—not by trying to make up your mind, but by simply looking at it, as one would study anything from a psychological distance—and then blending with and observing the natural setting. By varying from one focus (the decision) to another (the natural setting), you will avoid the trap of "trying too hard," and keep your mind fresh and open to intuitive insight.
- If you have brought with you a representation of your decision, at some point you may wish to conduct a brief ritual with this object. One client brought a different colored ribbon for each of his options, and then tied these to various trees. Then he sat for a time alternately looking at and considering each one.
- At some point, you will likely feel finished and ready to return from your quest. You may or may not feel that your decision has been made. While some people achieve a choice on the spot, many leave undecided, often to have their decision emerge a few hours, days, or even weeks later. Growing can take time.

Example: A thirty-something man I worked with couldn't decide whether to leave his job, which he loathed, and start his own business—a very risky proposition as he saw it—or stay put and continue trading personal misery for financial security.

For his quest, he choose a location and process involving considerable risk, despite my strongly expressed misgivings. He knew of a large lake in a state park, and he elected to swim across it in the dark of night. As he saw it, this quest closely paralleled the elements of his decision: to opt for security (stay on shore) or go for it (swim into darkness, uncertainty, and danger). He was a very good swimmer, so he believed he had the physical attributes necessary to complete his quest, but he was uncertain about his courage. As he told me later, the quest proved as frightening and meaningful as he had anticipated. When he reached the far shore, his decision was well in hand. Within three months, he was managing his own successful business. The power of this man's quest was a function of more than a physical challenge. As he told me, "After I got past my initial fear, the water and darkness didn't feel like enemies. The feel of it—being out there, just me and the elements—was almost a religious experience. I felt transformed."

Most quests need not involve such dramatic and potentially dangerous circumstances. When alone and relying upon the intellect, it is often difficult to *make* a decision, but in collaboration with the life force, it is usually possible to *grow* one.

NATURAL INTIMACY

*. . . Earth's the right place for love:
I don't know where it's likely to go better.*

Poet Robert Frost

Sex, which we flippantly refer to as "only natural," has become anything but. In fact, there may be no area of human behavior in which we are more confused and conflicted. Our culture and its media have made a mess of sexuality, associating it with violence, commercialism, politics, exploitation, and a host of other ills that have nothing to do with "lovemaking," as we call it. Trying to extract what is natural about sex from this jumbled mess has proven, to date, impossible for our society. A few individuals have found their way to healthy, loving sexual relationships, but with little help from the larger social disorder.

In search of the "natural" in sex, we turn to Dr. Ruth types, pornography, the flood of sexual imagery in media and advertising, erotic cinema and fiction, how-to books on lovemaking, the tall tales of our confidants, and promiscuous experimentation. But the messages are profoundly confusing. Some sources tell us to surrender to lust and hedonistic self-gratification, and never mind emotional intimacy. Others promote genuine love and commitment as prerequisites to sexual involvement. A few rail against sex as an instrument of evil. Still others concoct a witch's brew that mixes sex with violence, power, domination, pain, and exploitation. The result? Few of us know what a healthy sexual relationship feels like.

If we feel disconnected from the Earth, we are also estranged from our own animal constitution, and so, our sexual nature.

Because we no longer feel our animal nature, and because our culture and, too often, our parents do not speak clearly about sexuality, we are left to figure things out on our own. Mostly, we do this by fumbling and bumbling. We grapple to perform, and to live up to the mish-mash of cultural expectations about what "a good sex life" is. For many, sex is not an experience so much as a performance, and one we increasingly evaluate through measurement and comparison. How often should we have intercourse in a week? How many orgasms should we have in a session of lovemaking? How many times can we make love in one evening? Do we have multiple orgasms? Are we doing it the way they did it in that movie? Was this orgasm better than the last one?

Behind the quantification of sexual performance resides that ever-present question, the one that looms in the back of so many minds during lovemaking: "How am I doing?"

If you have to ask, you're probably not doing so hot.

In searching for what is natural in our sexuality, it should come as no surprise that the natural world has a great deal to teach us, certainly more than *The Joy of Sex*, and similar tomes. The Earth is inherently sexual, reproductive, sensory, and sensual. It is within nature that we discover the bedrock for all sexual experience—and that is *sensual* experience.

The basic lesson that the Earth has to teach us about sexuality is that sex isn't based on orgasm. It is based on sensuality. Orgasms are not a pathway to emotional and physical intimacy, but sensuality is. As an analogy, eating is not about feeling full. It is about nourishment. When we make the mistake of believing that eating is about getting full, then we eat too much, too little, and the wrong stuff for the wrong reasons. Similarly, sex is not about a chemical release. It is about immersion and absorption in emotional and sensory experience that, in turn, can lay the groundwork for mutual caring and loving intimacy.

When most of us think of sex, we envision a narrow band of physical behaviors with a distinct beginning and a peak conclusion—foreplay, arousal, and orgasm. But as anyone who is sensual and not merely sexual will report, sex begins far in advance of foreplay and persists well past orgasm. In fact, from a natural perspective, it is difficult if not impossible to discern where sex begins and where it concludes. For a truly sensual person, sex is a "movement" in a very long symphony of sensual experiences, and not an abrupt departure from one way of being into another.

If sex is actually an extension of sensuality, then lying in the lush grass under a shade tree on a hot day is sexual. Feeling the breeze run cool on one's sweat-soaked forehead is sexual. Listening to the cascading babble of a forest brook is sexual. Watching lightning split the black and blustery sky is sexual. Tasting a ripe cherry or raspberry is sexual. Smelling the aromas of a warm summer night is sexual.

An important part of the basis for a gratifying, caring sexual relationship rests upon each partner's capacity for sensual, not just sexual, absorption.

Some of us bypass sensuality in hot and rapid pursuit of orgasmic release, keeping track of our physical performance, carnal conquests, and the conduct of sexual politics; others shut down their sensuality, choking it with prudish repression and emotional inhibition. But whatever our poison, when we deny or circumvent our sensuality, we reject ourselves as animals, as organic creatures who relate to their environment and each other through their senses.

We use our senses not only to survive and function, but also to find one another, to touch, kiss, enjoy, taste, and smell each other, and to make contact across the sometimes wide emotional crevasses that separate one person from another. When we learn to become absorbed in pleasurable sensory experience, to relish the sensations of sight, sound, touch, taste, and smell, then we become sensual. When we do this lovingly with another human being, then we become intimately sexual.

Much of the repression of healthy sexuality that occurred in Western civilization for centuries grew from a cultural rejection of humans as sensual animals. At our furthest point of absurdity, humans were expected to have intercourse without sensual indulgence, sometimes without disrobing. By cutting off sexuality from sensual experience, society relegated it to other impersonations—procreation alone, domination, and power. When we divorced sexuality from our animal-based sensuality, we cut off its anchor, leaving it adrift.

That drifting has helped foster sex as an instrument of commercial advertising, sex as a power play, sex as violent pornography, sex as aberration, and all the other pretenders that masquerade as the real thing. When we are out of touch with the Earth's sensuality, as manifested in nature and in ourselves, we lose contact with what it means to be a sexual animal in a healthy sense.

Many who suffer from so-called sexual dysfunctions, such as psychologically mediated impotence, lack of sexual desire, and inability to experience orgasm, endure far more than a physical performance difficulty. They suffer from not feeling and not affirming their animal nature, or from being frightened by it. Others have retained their ability to perform, but have reduced their sexual nature to a mechanistic, task-oriented process designed to "produce" an orgasm. In either case, these folks have lost contact with their sensual roots, those that are given to us by the Earth.

There is a particularly poignant scene in the movie *Never Cry Wolf*, in which an American zoologist, dispatched to the wilds of Alaska to study the predatory habits of wolves, strips naked (save for his boots) on a warm August afternoon and lies in the tundra grass. While he sleeps, a herd of caribou encircle him, and, upon waking, he runs through them, looking for the wolves who are nearby and closing for the hunt. The sight of a "civilized" man lying unclothed in the grass and scrambling naked with wolves and caribou is an apt visual metaphor that strips away the artificial barriers we have constructed between ourselves and our innate animal nature. This zoologist, steeped in science and social propriety, becomes one more living entity in a sea of the same—wolves, mosquitoes, lichens, grasses, sky, and caribou. His body, lying naked against the living ground, bare to the sun and wind, is absorbed in the sensuality of the Earth. If you've had the privilege of lying naked on the ground, you know how sensual and sexual this can feel.

Ashamed, as most of us have been taught to be, of our nakedness, of the sounds, movements, and passionate abandon that accompany healthy, loving sexual intimacy, it is little wonder that so many people find sex dissatisfying or even repulsive. Granted, some unfortunate victims of rape, sexual abuse, and exploitation have more to contend with than becoming a sexual animal, but for many others a lost sense of sensuality is what thwarts their enjoyment and the achievement of emotional and physical closeness with their partners.

A couple I counseled about their lack of sexual intimacy typified this conundrum, as this case study illustrates:

"I'm not an animal," Ellen sizzled at me during our first session.

"With all due respect, Ellen . . . yes, you are," I replied.

Ellen and her husband, Tom, had never had a mutually satisfying sexual relationship during their six years of marriage. Ellen found herself unable to, as she put it, "let go" during lovemaking. Tom was incapable of responding to emotional sensitivity and intimacy, opting instead for mechanical performance. She hid from orgasm, while he pursued it with singular and compulsive purpose, as if it was the only thing about sex that mattered.

As Ellen described it, Tom's approach to making love was confined to "rubbing our bodies together." He acknowledged that this was largely true. Her approach was to "get it over with."

Ellen feared her animal nature. The meaning she attached to the word "animal" was derogatory to the point of revulsion. In her thinking, to be an animal was to be wild, uncontrolled, and savage. "What an animal!" we sometimes say about someone who is crude, filthy, cruel, or who makes no effort to disguise brazen, insensitive lust. In fact, such people are not being "animals" of the sort one finds in fields and forests. They are instead being humans at their worst.

Ironically, Tom embodied all of Ellen's stereotypes about being "an animal." His sexuality seemed confined to achieving the neurochemical release of orgasm. He lacked an awareness of his own or Ellen's sensuality, so his pursuit of sexual experience became mechanistic, self-centered, and insensitive.

"Having sex with Tom is like making love to a Neanderthal," Ellen shuddered.

"Sometimes when I approach Ellen about sex, I feel like I'm coming on to a nun," Tom complained.

"Your problem is not about sex," I told them. Both responded to my pronouncement with looks of disbelief.

"The problem is that you have lost your senses . . . quite literally. You don't know how to be with each other in a sensory, sensual way," I explained.

"I don't get it," Tom replied.

"Me either," Ellen echoed.

"It's nice to see you agreeing on something," I chuckled. "What I'm trying to say is that both of you must learn how to be sensual before you can become sexual in a loving way. I believe I know how you can do that, provided you're willing to do some odd stuff."

"You mean like in bed?" Ellen's eyes widened.

"Nope. I mean like outdoors," I answered.

"Outdoors? You mean like get it on in the woods or something?" Tom asked, already excited at the prospect.

"Sorry. Nothing like that. We'll start with simple things actually—rocks, leaves, flowers, and berries," I explained.

Ellen's disgust for sex, and Tom's insensitivities toward it, while not the result of earlier abuse or assault, were so entrenched that it was a long and painstaking effort to persuade them to rediscover their sensual capacities through contact with nature. Anyone who has made love in a field or forest can attest to the heightened sensuality that accompanies sex in close proximity to the Earth; however, Tom was far too eager and Ellen far too reluctant for so bold a course.

Instead, I suggested they begin by simply touching the natural world (which is, again, a sexual world) in a sensual manner, initially using tactile explorations of stones, flower petals, moss, leaves, sand, and other non-animal entities. This is a well established psychological method called "sensate focusing"—concentrating, in this instance, on one's tactile sensations. The objectives were to desensitize Ellen's fears of sensual experience (again, the basis of sexuality) and to sensitize Tom to the non-orgasmic aspects of touching.

From there, they progressed to other kinds of sensory absorption, such as the aroma of wild flowers and herbs, the taste of wild berries and nuts, the visual qualities of all these and many other physical things, and the sounds of waterfalls, bird calls, wind, and surf. Essentially, Tom and Ellen took long, unhurried baths in their senses, learning to rediscover the sensory basis of their animal natures, which is the bedrock of sexuality.

Gradually, Ellen's animal constitution reawakened, while Tom's broadened from its narrow, orgasmic focus. As their sensory explorations with the Earth brought them closer to the meeting point of true sensuality, I recommended that they begin gradually exploring their sensual, rather than sexual, relationship. They shifted from the less threatening arena of sensual contact with nature to the more apprehensive realm of their physical relationship. So-called "non-sexual touching" was the next step, which they undertook in fields and forests—away from other people, of course. Sensual contact between caring people is greatly enhanced when they are surrounded by the beauty and innate eroticism of the natural world. Soon, their desire for outright sexual contact welled up from these sensual experiences.

"You told us no sex for now," Ellen said at a subsequent session.

"That's right. I want you to focus on sensual interaction," I replied.

"Well, we both feel ready . . . for sex, I mean," Ellen continued.

"Yeah. It's different between us now," Tom interjected.

"How?" I asked.

"You know how some people just scarf down their food and never really taste it or enjoy it?" Tom began. "Well, that's how I used to be with sex, but now I feel things that I didn't before. It's tough to explain, but I guess you could say I've become a gourmet instead of a meat and potatoes guy."

"He's really able to feel more. He's sensitive, not just to me, but to himself, too," Ellen added.

"And what about you?" I asked Ellen.

"I feel more too. I'm not as afraid of letting go, of getting into the sensations. I think we're ready," she concluded.

Once again, Ellen and Tom wanted each other as people—as loving, erotic animals, not just reproductive organs or folds of skin.

The rebirth of this couple's sexuality was built on a foundation of immersion in the sensual experiences afforded by the Earth, not upon direct sexual interactions with each other, which came much later in their healing process. They did not learn about healthy and fulfilling sex by engaging in unhealthy and frustrating sex, as so many of us attempt to do through promiscuous and performance-driven exploits, but rather by engaging in sensual absorption. From the latter, sexuality flows quite naturally.

Our senses play a fundamental role in our sexual development and its behavioral expression, and these same senses (touching, tasting, smelling, and seeing) are grounded in our experience of nature. It is our animal nature that has, through evolutionary development, granted us these sensing capacities, as well as all the physical aspects and drives associated with our sexuality. Before some of us can be sexual animals, we must re-learn what it means to be *sensual* animals, and that is what Tom and Ellen accomplished.

In our animal nature we will find the essential elements that comprise our sexual lives—the capacity to be an expressive individual, to be unafraid to reveal feelings, and to reside first and foremost in the certainty of being a sensing, physical creature. This animal nature, which sustains and enlivens sexuality, is part of a broader expressiveness—of remembering to howl at the moon, to do cartwheels in the grass, to make angels in the snow, to pound fists on the ground, to cry in the rain, to laugh when the wind messes our hair, to eat the Earth's good foods ravenously, and to move and moan and revel in each other's loving touches.

That's being an animal.

Be one.

EXERCISE:

CEREMONY OF SENSUALITY

While sensual (and, therefore, sexual) awareness can be enhanced in a variety of ways, contact with nature is, in my experience and that of many of my clients, the most powerful and rapid approach.

- Identify objects or processes in nature that are rich in sensory qualities, and that are pleasing and appealing to you. In particular, these should be conducive to touching and smelling.
- Spend time, either alone or as a couple (as your situation warrants), focusing your senses on these natural elements. This type of concentration is *sensory*. Use your primary physical senses, not your intellect, to gather sensual information about the object.
- Most often, it is helpful to begin with your tactile sense (touching), and to use smaller objects that can be held in your hand, handled with your fingers, or rubbed over your skin. Smooth stones, flowers, moss, sand, and leaves are commonly used.
- From there you may wish to progress to aromatic objects. Smell is a primary determinant in sexual arousal. These should be things that you find pleasing—perhaps flowers, honey, herbs, pine needles, cedar, freshly mown hay, and the like.
- Whether touching or smelling, it is important that you deeply immerse your senses in the natural object. Your sensory study should be thorough and intense. You will know you have succeeded in this ceremony when you begin to experience *sensual* arousal. Your senses will become more acute, enjoyable, and absorbent, as they should be during lovemaking.
- Couples may wish to help each other develop sensual awareness through mutual sensory immersion. They may want to rub an object over each other, such as a smooth, round stone, for example. This helps some couples to make the transition from the sensual ceremony being an individual process to an interactive one.

- Tactile immersion may also prove helpful. Slipping into warm water, lying on warm sand or earth, or spreading out on grass or prairie can amplify a "whole body" sensual acuity.

For those who are experiencing difficulties in their sexual relationships, sensuality should be enhanced before once again resuming outright lovemaking. Working through the ceremony of sensuality first as individuals and then as a couple is most effective.

CHAPTER
FIFTEEN

MIRROR, MIRROR

A man does not seek to see himself in running water,
but in still water.
For only what is itself still can impart stillness into others.

Chinese Philosopher Chuang-tse

"What do you believe in? What are your values?" I asked Carol.

A murky blend of consternation, confusion and sadness filled her face. It is a look I have often seen, not just on other people, but in my own mirror.

"I know what other people *want* me to believe in. I know what values they want me to have, but I'm not sure which values are my own and which have been imposed on me by others," she replied.

Few of us are. The things we value in life are commonly a mixture of what we believe in our hearts to be important and worth living for, and what our family, social community, and culture want us to believe in. We receive constant messages from family, friends, and co-workers about how they want and expect us to live. When we run counter to these expectations and the values upon which they rest, there is often interpersonal hell to pay.

One of the vital tasks of life is determining one's own values and clearly delineating them from those given to us by others. This process is central to distinguishing one's self from the other people

101

who populate one's life. When we fail to effectively separate ourselves from the social milieu in which we live and don't stake out our own psychological territory, we end up losing track of who we are in the pea soup of family and personal relationships. Unhappiness often follows. Psychologists call the process of distinguishing one's self from others "individuation," but it isn't something we do once, in adolescence or early adulthood, and then forget about. Over a lifetime, most of us return periodically to search our souls and rediscover who we are, what we believe in, and whether our lives reflect those beliefs or mock them.

For the mind to clearly understand itself is somewhat like an eye trying to see itself—virtually impossible. Consequently, many of us attempt to clarify our values and our sense of self by talking and interacting with other people, using them as mirrors in which we can more accurately perceive who we are. Sometimes using other folks for self-reflection works fine, particularly if those people want us to be a unique individual, rather than some imitation. A good listener or friend who cares enough to let us become who we truly are is a rare but wonderful gift. But, too often, when we share what we believe with important folks in our lives, they find something they don't quite like or that threatens them, or they take sides with one part of ourselves against another, only reinforcing our inner conflicts and confusions. Then they suggest that we shouldn't feel a certain way, or that we should believe in and value certain things that we don't. They profess to know what is best for us. In short, they reject rather than reflect.

What's so bad about that? It all depends upon how the process is conducted. For instance, if I take the time to explore and understand the inherent nature of my daughter, and if I exercise care in distinguishing what I want for her from what she wants for herself, then I can reasonably lobby her to adopt certain values; such as sensitivity to others, assertiveness, and respect for the environment. Provided that I honor and affirm who she is, as distinct from me, then she will have the opportunity to be herself and, at the same time, try on my values to determine if they weave well with her own. She must also, however, have the freedom to reject my values, and I must have the courage and trust to respect her decision.

As any parent knows, this can be a risky business, and there's no guarantee that one's trust in a child will pay off in the long run. Sometimes it does not. But when we attempt to force-feed someone our values while ignoring or negating their own, there is little or no hope that they will be better off for our efforts.

Carol had suffered a great deal of force-feeding from other people. She got caught up in the crazy, circuitous dance of trying to please important folks in her life. She would tell them what they wanted to hear, and then they would expect to hear more of the same from her. When she realized that she was being the person others wanted her to be and not her true self, she tried to set matters straight by revealing the real McCoy. Trouble was, nobody wanted her to be real. They had grown accustomed to the fake Carol, not the genuine one. Consequently, she experienced frequent rejection, and tremendous pressure to be the person they wanted her to be.

"I can't figure out who I am. I try listening to my own inner voice, but I'm not sure how much is my own and how much is a recording of other people's ideas," she confessed.

"You may find it helpful to be alone," I advised. "Well, not actually alone, but away from people."

"What do you mean . . . not actually alone?"

"I mean it may help to spend time with your source in nature, with your Mother, the Earth," I explained.

"What good will that do?" she asked.

"She accepts us as we are. After all, she gave us our basic nature. We came from her." I struggled to be understood.

"I'm not sure I follow. It sounds a little too New Age for me," she replied.

"It does, but whatever you think about my oddball ideas, I think it would help you to insulate yourself from other people, including me, so that you can clearly hear your inner voice," I suggested.

"I can buy that," she agreed.

For millennia, people have wandered off into natural and wild places to find themselves. These personal quests are an honored tradition in many tribal and native cultures, even in the Judeo-Christian lineage that has so shaped mainstream American society. Jesus trekked into the wilderness, struggling with Satan and his own dark side. Buddha sequestered himself from human influences and worldly pleasures and meditated until he attained enlightenment. The initiation rites of many tribes required that young people go off alone into the wilds, hopefully to discover their true nature.

While Carol had little interest in finding nirvana or ascending to holy status, she did feel the virtually universal need to perceive her core, her essential self.

Regrettably, it often isn't safe for a woman to go off alone in the wilderness these days, though some still do. Carol would have spent all her time and energy modulating her fears, so instead I suggested that she visit a retreat center in northeast Iowa. There, she would have the benefit of austere but safe lodging, a social milieu that guarded each person's privacy, and the run of hundreds of acres of farm fields, prairie, a small lake, and woodlands.

These days, many so-called retreats are built around interacting with people rather than nature. For instance, many addiction recovery and personal growth programs seek to use social intercourse as a conduit for emotional healing and individuation. Sometimes these are very helpful, particularly if we are at a stage where social affirmation and feedback are what we lack. And there are people who can teach us how to approach the Earth to gain self-awareness, but they usually realize that each of us requires solitude to complete this process, so they facilitate this aloneness rather than insisting that we slavishly listen to their guidance. Eventually, discovering or revisiting one's true self requires the quiet solitude afforded by the natural environment.

So it was for Carol.

"After the first day, which was tough, I found myself getting very quiet inside. I guess it helped that it was quiet outside, too. You were right, though. Being outdoors helped me see myself more clearly," she told me upon her return.

"How so?" I asked.

"Trying to see myself was like standing in a pool of water and looking down at my reflection on the surface. If there are lots of people in the pool with me, or if I'm rushing around, the surface is all rough and wavy and I can't see much. But when it's just me and nature, the water gets calm and my reflection gets clearer," she explained.

"That's a good metaphor," I replied.

"But there was something else, too. I didn't really feel alone. It was like what you said about the Earth being our Mother. I began feeling like I had gone home somehow. It sounds weird, but home is supposed to be where you can just hang out, where nobody will bother you, and you get accepted for who you are. That's how I felt," she added.

"Who accepted you?" I asked.

"I accepted myself, I suppose, but I also felt like life was accepting me. I felt like I belonged, like I fit, that it was okay with life for me to go ahead and be who I am, even if some people can't handle that."

Carol had found the focus she sought. She found it nature's way.

Not everyone who seeks a sense of self by going home to the Earth comes away with Carol's renewed clarity and self-affirmation. I've sent clients on such quests who had very taxing times. Some were too fidgety to immerse themselves in the experience, others couldn't abide the lack of social contact, and a few found rain, snow, or bugs too much to tolerate. But many others returned with still inner waters and the clear reflection of self that Carol discovered.

I have undertaken a number of these solitary quests myself, most recently in the Badlands and Black Hills of South Dakota. These sojourns can be uncomfortable, despite the benefit of clarifying one's values and sense of self. It would be a mistake to delude ourselves with images of paradise lost, blissful communion with nature, and life-shaking visions. Quests can be tough, both emotionally and physically, and the lessons learned may not be startling or immediate. Sometimes this sort of learning takes months to incubate before giving birth to something new in our person.

This seems to be the price the Earth demands for the benefit of her wisdom.

Quests of this kind do not require days or weeks holed up in caves, retreat centers, monasteries, or the wilderness. Brief interludes of solitary communion with the Earth can be enlightening, as well. Even half an hour of such time calms the turbulent waters of the psyche and permits a clearer reflection of self to emerge. Some of my clients have adopted this as a daily ritual, either in the morning before the busy day's tentacles have taken hold, or in the evening when frenetic activity is ebbing away.

104

The search for self and the endeavor to illuminate one's values leads many of us to other people and resources—gurus, experts, academicians, our elders, books, workshops, support groups, and all the other "show me the way" guidance systems that our culture has created. The fact that we rely more upon each other and the social order than upon the ageless wisdom of the Earth and its natural order tells us how alienated we have become from our source. Ours is one of the first cultures to turn away en masse from the solace and sagacity of the Earth, and to overlook her as a counselor when we feel confused and troubled.

It shows.

Despite the psychologizing of our culture, many of us remain abjectly muddled about who we are, why we are, and, as in Carol's instance, what we stand for. Like the good parent she is, the Earth will let us be who we truly are while in her presence, and she will even show us our true self.

"There's one other thing," Carol told me before we concluded our final session.

"What's that?"

"One afternoon at the retreat center while I was sitting by the pond, I saw one of the swans float by. Its reflection on the water was clear, but even though it was looking right at its own reflection, it didn't seem to notice itself," she began.

"Yes?" I urged her on.

"I thought about how lucky that swan was, not having to contemplate its own image, and not having to wonder what it believes in or how it should act. It doesn't need to see its reflection. It just gets to be what it is . . . a swan," she concluded.

I waited a moment while she stirred that idea around.

"Carol, maybe that wasn't just a swan," I suggested.

"What do you mean?"

"That swan is closer to the Earth than you or I. It lives its life in constant and intimate contact with the life force." I was taking her a few more mental steps.

"So?"

"So maybe it was showing you something you needed to see," I finished, not wanting to lead her any farther.

Carol left perplexed by my mysterious narrative, and a tad miffed that I hadn't just handed over my conclusion outright, but, like Mr. Cavanaugh, I'm not a lifeguard, just a swimming instructor. I had to trust that she would find her own meaning in there somewhere, and she did. A few months later, I got a brief note from Carol in the mail.

"Philip . . . You were right about the swan. She was a messenger of sorts. She showed me that once you've seen yourself clearly, you don't need to keep looking over and over, constantly trying to figure yourself out. Just be who you are. Thanks . . . Carol."

That's what the Earth does for us.

She helps us clearly see who we are.

Then we can let ourselves be.

E X E R C I S E :

CEREMONY OF REFLECTION

Each of us is subjected to a persistent flood of messages about who we are, what we should believe in, and how to conduct our existence. Living in the world requires that at least some of these be given heed; however, it is essential that we balance these outer voices with the wisdom of our inner voice. Tuning in to one's intuition and inner mental mirror requires quieting or temporarily escaping the messages from people, media, and society. For most of us, daily life has too much "signal noise" to distill one's inner voice from all the other hullabaloo.

- Find a place in nature that is free from most human noise and activity. You don't need to be a purist about this. Even a relatively quiet park or wayside can suffice.
- Assume a posture that is sufficiently comfortable that you can stay in it for ten minutes or more without having to shift around. Lying down is often best.
- Surveying your surroundings, take a few deep, easy breaths. Imagine yourself breathing in the natural scene in front of you, whether it is quiet, stormy, cold or warm. Then as you exhale, imagine you are breathing out all the cluttered thoughts in your mind. Take a few minutes to breathe in the natural world and breathe out the stale, thought-cluttered air in your head.
- Once you feel that your mind has been cleared of most of those outside, human-made messages, close your eyes and tune in to your inner atmosphere. Your inner being feels clearer, less complicated, and more at peace.
- At this point, if you want to hear your voice, as distinct from those of the outer world, you can ask yourself a question. This question could range from the pragmatic ("Do I want to find another job?") to the existential ("What is most important to me in life?"). Some of my clients find it helpful to ask their questions by saying them out loud, but softly.
- Upon asking your question, remain still and quiet inside

until an "answer" (in whole or part) emerges from within you. This answer may come as an inner voice, a mental image, an emotion, a memory, or some other symbol or representation. It may come immediately, or at some point later on when you aren't expecting it. Some questions may require more than one episode of reflection and may need to be "grown," as I have eluded to previously, over a period of time.

Of course, the ceremony of reflection does not have to be performed in a natural setting. Experience has taught me, however, that nature's presence enhances its power and fulfillment. Perhaps this is because in nature it is easier to let go of the need to be doing and having, and instead to embrace a state of being.

CREATION

*If we have powers of imagination, these are activated by
the magic display of color and sound, of form and movement, such as we observe in the clouds of the sky, the
trees and bushes and flowers, the waters and the wind,
the singing birds, and the movement of the great blue
whale through the sea.*

Author Thomas Berry

While we often marvel at the creativity of
our species, we easily forget the rootstock of
our inspiration. Our magnificent achievements in music, painting, dance, poetry,
architecture, science, photography, pottery,
and other creative forms rest upon the
dream-like spells that nature casts upon us
when we are in her presence.

The ability to express one's inner self
through an artistic or creative mode is central
to emotional well-being. From the classical
composer to the backyard banjo strummer,
from the world class sculptor to the basement
wood carver, and from the finest watercolor master
to the toddler scribbling with a crayon, each of us requires a way to
take that invisible essence that we feel in our soul and bring it into the
world of form and expression. When we do so, we participate in the
ongoing mystery of creation, of which we are a small part. By express-
ing our inner nature, which has been given us by our Mother, the
Earth, we join her in the sacred accomplishment of birth, and so bring
new forms and possibilities into the world.

When I work with clients whose powers of creativity have slipped away, it is apparent that they have little capacity to engage with life, or to employ the verve necessary for their own emotional healing. The life force does not flow through them, but rather is blocked somewhere. Peter, a burned-out businessman who came to me for "depression," was a prime example.

"I need to get my life together," he told me.

"How would you propose to do that?" I asked.

"I need to improve my relationship with my wife, spend more quality time with my kids, manage things better at work, take a more positive attitude toward life, quit worrying so much . . . things like that," he replied, each word laden with effort.

"Those are a lot of changes. They'll probably require a fair amount of energy and creativity to pull off. After all, you're talking about re-creating large portions of your life. Are you feeling creative?" I inquired.

"Do I look creative?" Peter replied, not even able to laugh at his own joke.

"Frankly, you look like the living dead."

Living richly requires considerable dynamism and imagination. Growing changes in one's life requires even more. As a psychotherapist, I've sent too many clients out on a mission of rebirth without first considering whether the wellspring of their imagination had gone dry. I don't do that anymore. Even therapists learn from their experiences. Before tackling the business of growing changes or decisions, bringing new life to relationships, or attempting to overhaul any significant aspect of someone's existence, one must first prime the pump.

People whose imaginations have gone into a spiritual coma are in no shape to transform old patterns, bad habits, and entrenched moods. And without the energy necessary to fuel new ways of living in the world, there is little hope of bringing forth regeneration.

As a modern adage goes, "If you always do what you've always done, then you'll always get what you've always gotten." If one lacks the capacity to dream, imagine, play, immerse in natural wonder, open the mind, and experiment (aspects of creativity), then one will keep getting the same old results.

Sadly, for many of us, getting the same old results has become a way of life. We shuffle through our daily forced marches like robots, mouthing the same sentences, performing the same behaviors in compulsive sequence, rerunning the same thoughts and opinions, watching the same TV shows, driving to work the same way, going to the same restaurants, and doing our utmost to minimize surprises, variety, and spontaneous upwellings. Then, when our lives are knocked off kilter by tragedy, unwanted change, emotional symptoms like depression or anxiety, or any of the wrecking balls that can career through our existence, we find ourselves with few adaptive resources. We keep using our old ways of behaving and feeling, wrongly supposing that if they worked once, they will surely work again. Often they do not.

In the natural world, creativity is not a skill or an artistic expression. It is the modus operandi. The life force *is* creativity. Anyone who has seen a plant robustly growing on the rocky, cold face of an alpine cliff realizes just how imaginative, resourceful, and tenaciously creative life can be. Our Earth Mother has devised organisms that exist in utter darkness under incredible atmospheric pressure in the farthest depths of her oceans. She has brought forth plants, animals, insects, microbes, and geologic elements that display an almost infinite variety of shapes, colors, and functions. Her spectrum of sounds, pigments, and textures contains nuances no artist, photographer, or musician has ever duplicated. She does it all.

The Earth is an ongoing creation, intensely expressive, artistic, highly experimental, into risk-taking, and ripe with possibilities and playfulness. There is no finer mentor for creativity and imagination, and those of us who have gone into hibernation in this regard will do well to apprentice ourselves to nature. There is no end to what we can learn, to how we can be inspired, and to where our flights of fancy can carry us if we immerse ourselves in the ebbs and flows of the life force.

But how does one lead someone like Peter to understand this? I elected to try hands-on experience.

"Get a good microscope and some fresh pond water," I told him.

"Pond water?" Peter grunted, incredulous.

"Right. Then sketch what you see under the microscope," I added.

"Look, I took biology 101 a long time ago. I don't need to study paramecium. I need some sound advice about how to put my life back in order." He seemed understandably miffed.

"With all due respect, you've got all the order you need. Probably a lot more than you need. A little imaginative *disorder* might be therapeutic at this point," I added.

He eyed me awhile and then cracked a bit of a smile.

"Okay. We'll do it your way this one time, but I don't get how this is going to help me," he said.

"I know. That's why you came to someone like me. You don't get it," I replied.

So Peter did as I asked, even if grudgingly. However, shortly he discovered that, biology 101 notwithstanding, he still found those tiny creatures under the lens quite fascinating. What's more, so did his kids, who gathered round to help dad with his odd experiment. Pretty soon his wife was squinting at those weird little bugs as well. Before long, the pond water was replaced by flower pollen, blades of grass, sand, some dust from on top of the refrigerator, a feather, one of mom's hairs, and everything else they could think of that would fit under that lens.

Upon his return for our next session, Peter threw his sketch pad on the coffee table in front of me.

"There, just like you asked," he smiled.

"Not bad," I critiqued, flipping the pages. "What else?"

"What do you mean, 'What else?'," he snorted.

"What else happened?" I said.

Peter quit playing tough. He leaned forward, folded his hands, and cleared his throat, looking at the African violet on the table.

"Something. I'm different somehow. Not sure just how yet, and I'm not even sure it had anything to do with that microscope thing, but I feel some sort of new juices flowing, if you will," he replied.

"Well, let's not jump to any conclusions," I suggested. "How about if we just give something else a try?"

"Okay," he perked up a bit. "Lay it on me."

"You ever play any musical instruments?" I asked.

"Yeah, the drums. I was in band in high school, and then in college I played with a rock group for a couple years."

"Drums? Super. I want you to drum the sunset sometime next week," I said.

"Drum the sunset," he repeated. "How the hell does somebody drum a sunset?"

"I suggest you get a Native American drum. Then you just sit outside where you have a good view of the sunset and translate the feeling of what you are seeing into the sound of the drum," I explained.

Peter stared back in absolute stupefaction. I may as well have asked him to stand on his head and whistle "Bridge Over the River Kwai" during his company's next board meeting.

"Did I lose you somewhere, Peter?" I chimed in after a long silence.

"No way. This is too far out. What is this, some sort of warrior weekend technique or something? Have you been reading too much Robert Bly, or what?" he shot back.

"Robert Bly didn't invent drumming," I replied. "Look, if it's too much of a stretch for you, why not take one of your kids along and let him start you off?"

After 30 minutes of reframing, repackaging, and demystifying, I convinced Peter to drum the sunset with his nine-year-old son's assistance. As it happened, the boy made short work of Peter's prideful reticence, quickly drawing him into the spontaneous creation of impromptu sound out of visual inspiration. They had a blast. By the third evening, Peter had purchased a second drum for his son and was under intense pressure to let his wife come along.

Over the next few weeks, we primed Peter's creative pump with a variety of Earth-inspired activities involving clay sculpting, wood carving, building sand castles, and painting with watercolors. Gradually, the burned-out businessman became a revved-up Homo Sapien. With the juices once again flowing, Peter was able to turn his renewed energies toward the pragmatic difficulties that had rendered him close to ashes in the first place, and with considerable success. Had he attacked these worldly problems without first restoring his freshness and creative verve, there is little chance he would have bettered his circumstances.

Living well is an ongoing act of creation.

In some deeply existential sense that few of us consciously perceive and appreciate, we are born again each day and presented with the challenge of creating ourselves anew. If we are bonded with the Earth, our chances for a daily rebirth of sorts, minor or major, are much greater.

When we create, we give birth to new possibilities, and so become like the Earth.

Reborn, again and again.

EXERCISE:

CEREMONY OF CREATION

When our creativity runs dry, the Earth offers a wellspring of new inspiration, play, and energetic exploration. By activating our creative energies, we can apply ourselves more effectively to a broad expanse of productive areas, such as music, design, problem-solving, writing, parenting, business development and, of course, fun. Our Earth Mother offers a rich venue in which to prime our creative pumps.

- Gather some items from the natural world—stones, twigs, leaves, pine cones, sea or snail shells, seeds, and so on.
- Place these objects in front of you. Sit quietly, taking a few fresh draws of air to clear your mind.
- Turning your awareness to the natural objects, begin to play with them, creating different designs, juxtapositions, and forms. There is no need for any of these creations to make sense or to conform to some preconceived notion of what is "right." In fact, you may find this ceremony more helpful if you allow the form, whatever it may be, to create itself, so to speak, through you, rather than the other way around. The important element, however, is to play, not work.
- Whatever you create, start over when the form feels finished. Rearrange the items as many times as you like and, if possible, become more free and outlandish in your creations with each new playful effort.
- A variation on this ceremony is to work with a single item or element. Sand is popular in this regard, as are pebbles, sticks, and flowers. A uniform object or substance may require more creative imagination.
- If all of this seems like gobbledygook to you, ask a child for assistance. Have the child go through the ceremony, and then watch how she or he takes to the task. Children are wonderful teachers in this regard.

There are, of course, many other ways to stimulate and apply creative energy in concert with the Earth. A great deal of music, painting, photography, and writing are inspired by our Mother, so if you have an inclination in any of these arenas, they may offer a strong ceremonial venue. It is possible to "write" a sunset, waterfall, thunderstorm, or other natural event, either through poetry or descriptive verse. One can "play" nature's beauty and power through musical instruments. Whatever your form and method, the Earth is rich with creativity, and you can readily share in this to reawaken your own generative powers.

EARTH TIME

"Why are you rushing so much?" asked the Rabbi.
"I'm rushing after my livelihood," the man answered.
"And how do you know," said the Rabbi, "that your
livelihood is running on before you, so that you have to
rush after it? Perhaps it's behind you, and all you need
to do is stand still."

Poet T.S. Eliot

I had been paddling hard for over an hour, snaking through a chain of lakes in northern Minnesota connected by fast-running streams and more sedate channels. Finally, I found a broad cove devoid of cabins, boat launches, or other imprints of human habitation. In residence here were sprawling carpets of aquatic plants festooned with yellow and white water lilies, tall and slender reed grass, and marshy shores with overhanging birch and cedar. The early morning sun carved bright reflections on the shallow bottom and splashed mirrored illuminations off the water's surface onto the nearby shore.

As I glided the canoe quietly into this sanctuary, a pair of loons cavorted 50 yards off my port quarter, pursuing each other in mock battle, part flying and part running across the surface. The long, curving neck of a great blue heron slid out from behind a tuft of shore grass. Soon it was in flight, squawking at my intrusion, no matter how benign.

This seemed a perfect place to immerse myself in that rare activity—if one can call it an activity—commonly known as "drifting."

115

I placed my paddle aboard, slid down onto the flotation cushion on the canoe floor, hung my head over the starboard side, peered down at the slowly passing bottom, and drifted. There was a finicky breeze that came in little bursts and rushed away, leaving tightly spaced ripples on the otherwise flat surface. It turned the canoe one way and then another, sometimes in full circles, or back and forth like an ambivalent watch hand. But it was all out of my control, which was my intent.

While our Earth Mother is capable of intensely focused energy and cataclysmic mayhem, she also knows how to kick back and while away the hours, an approach to passing time that few of us employ. Her sense of order is more languid than our own. She is not driven by schedules, tasks, and timelines. She makes things up as she goes along. She progresses, to be sure, but also rests and plays, while too many of our species move through the hours of each day like soldiers on a forced march.

Cultural expectations to the contrary, we are not made to run at breakneck speed for hours, days, and years on end. While humans are not tortoises, neither are they cheetahs (which mostly sprint and then rest anyway). It is not in our nature, as derived from the natural world, to be always moving, on task, and hard at it.

The human experience of time's movement is measured by the brain's inner clock, a psychological timepiece that frequently fails to correlate with the ones we wear on our wrists and hang on our walls. Each of us experiences time individually, no matter what our watches say. When I conduct workshops on stress, I often ask participants to close their eyes and estimate the passage of one minute (no counting, of course), and to raise their hands when they think 60 seconds have passed. So far, the shortest "minute" on record is 11 seconds, and the longest is over 100 seconds. It doesn't matter what the clocks say. What matters is how each of us feels time passing. When we experience it at breakneck speed (11 seconds is a fast minute), all our physiological and psychological systems are racing to keep up, and losing all the while.

The actual experience of time passing and, therefore, of one's life passing, is not determined by the movements of a watch hand or the markings on a calendar. If I move through life at the rate of 11-second minutes, then my years pass very quickly. For example, 80 years of 11-second minutes feels much shorter than 80 years of 100-second minutes, even though the calibrations on the calendar are the same. My minutes in the canoe in the embrace of one of nature's summer afternoons felt much longer than those I spend rushing about in my everyday life.

In the medium-sized human services business I manage, there are sometimes relentless demands on the time and energy of employees, leaving little space for drifting. But having learned a lesson from the natural world in this regard, we strive within our corporate culture to encourage "goofing off," as we call it. Employees are not criticized or passed over for advancement because they take the time to joke, or to sit by the trees and flowers in the front of our building. They're not punished because they go home a little early sometimes or spontaneously take an afternoon off.

Goofing off is essential to creativity and to productivity, and to living one's life rather than blazing through it at the mental speed of light.

We don't become more inventive and fruitful by shoving our noses so far into the grindstone that we sheer them off. The Earth is the prime example of that principle. The almost limitless creativity and bountiful productivity of the life force is spawned within the meandering and seemingly aimless drifting of time and events in the natural world.

The Earth has taken hundreds of millions of years to evolve some of her experiments, including our own species. And while individual humans are not blessed with the luxury of long epochs, there is much we can create within our allotted years provided we don't rush too quickly.

Stress and burnout are the common cold of the modern mind, and we won't find a tonic in some glib prescription for relaxation training, time management, or setting priorities. The cure is just outside your door. Our Earth Mother knows more about kicking back than all the stress management sages on the planet, and she charges far less. The only expense is a little bit of your time.

Moving from human time to Earth time involves passing through a temporal warp, but you don't need an atomic-powered Delorean or an H. G. Wells time machine. The warp, or transitional plane, is present wherever one can pass from the noisy, rapid-fire world of modern human invention to the quiet, patient places of the Earth.

One of the most pronounced ways to experience this kind of time travel is to walk into a field of tall corn. Once well within its confines, all the mayhem and mania of modern existence fades. One is surrounded by sturdy, vibrant life. The air wafting through the stalks is pungent with the aroma of living things, not the stale smut of exhaust and emissions. The sounds are of wind tickling tassels and greens, and human noises, if any, are muffled and distant. The footing is forgiving and warm, not bruising and unyielding. But most of all, time seems to slow. Perhaps it actually does.

The relative motion of objects is intricately related to one's perception of time, as Einstein asserted. When we and all manner of objects in our vicinity are moving about at a rapid pace, we experience time passing quickly. Slow one's relative motion and that of surrounding things, and time is perceived as passing at a more leisurely gait. Most often, Earth time is slower than human time, for the simple reason that nature is usually more unhurried about motion and change. When we visit, we can partake of slower and more graceful minutes, hours, and days.

Time elongates. The experience of life stretches.

When we place ourselves within our Earth Mother's enfolding arms, we feel the timeless quality of the natural world's unhurried movements, the same movements that have worked patiently for eons to bring about the unending emergence of the life force in all the planet's creatures and processes. There is no hurry. All will be done in good time. And when we slip into Earth time and out of the warp speed pace of human time, we enjoy the same experience of flow and ease that grows the walnut tree, lets fall the whispering brook, stretches out the yawning lion in the shade, evolves a species over millions of years, and moves each Homo Sapiens from fetus to child to adult to dust.

The Earth has time.

We may not.

But we can borrow time from her.

BRETHREN

At times almost all of us envy the animals. They suffer and die, but do not seem to make a "problem" of it.

Philosopher Alan Watts

It had been one of those days that seems to suck the marrow out of one's soul. The collective demands of deadlines, phones calls, and dozens of unpredictable, disruptive events had left me rattled and spent. Looking out my fourth floor window at the interstate highway that slices through the hill just north of my building, I rubbed my face and took a deep breath.

I glanced at the digital clock on my computer monitor, and then down at the strip malls, restaurants, motels, and gas stations that have eaten much of the prairie that once surrounded the building where I labor. The remaining field of grass below my window seemed to struggle against the encircling concrete and asphalt, but clearly it was in retreat.

"What a dump," I mumbled, exhaling the day's stress.

Idly, I glanced down at a wooden billboard recently erected next to the highway. There I was pleasantly surprised to see two red-tailed hawks perched atop one end of the sign, surveying the steady stream of freeway traffic a few dozen yards away. Set amidst the busy, developed surroundings, this pair seemed an island of the natural in a sea of the unnatural.

They sat there, scanning the environment for some time, and as I watched them, I began to leave the human-made madness of my day behind. In a matter of minutes the sight of these magnificent birds lifted my spirit out of its dour funk. Soon, it was as if I were being pulled out to them, away from the person-made, techno-driven, helter-skelter surroundings that most of us have come to regard as our normal habitat. Our winged brethren presented me with a measure of freedom and emotional respite; they reminded me that amidst all the grating noise, spewing gas and ugly eyesores of human invention, nature still lives. The force that gave all of us life still surrounds us with a tenaciously peaceful presence.

It is no meaningless quirk of human nature that most of us will turn away from almost anything we are doing to catch a glimpse of a wild animal. A deer standing frozen in a cluster of trees, a hawk perched on a fence post, a rabbit sniffing the wind, a fish jumping from a still pond, a butterfly flitting across a flowered field, a chipmunk scurrying beneath the porch—each creature draws our attention with a quiet call to our souls. Despite its subtlety, this call is louder than a blaring television, a flashing marquee or a color-splashed billboard. Unlike all the other "voices" that grab seductively and rudely at our awareness, our brethren creatures are not out to sell us something, take charge of our senses, or influence how we live our lives or see the world.

They simply are.

Life, it has been said, may be roughly divided into three broad categories of existential experience . . . doing, having, and being. While in a state of doing, we are performing some task. People do homework, lawn mowing, computer programming, house cleaning, report writing, committee meetings, manual labor, yes, even windows. The defining aspect of a state of doing is an activity focused on some end, some goal. Doers are task-oriented.

In America, a lot of doing is directed toward having—the acquisition of stuff, status, power, and attention. Money, houses, titles, cars, influence, promotions, diplomas—all these things and situations are the accouterments of having. Doing and having tend to go together for most of us. We do in order to have and, too often, in order to justify our own existence. The more we do the more we have, and the more valuable we are, or so our culture tells us. But when the dust has settled after another frenetic day of doing, what do we actually have?

Everything but the experience of being.

If you'll run a quick review of your waking day and determine roughly how much time you spend engaged in doing or having, chances are there isn't much left over for just being. In fact, being is an odd and unfamiliar state for most of us. Take away doing and having, and most folks figure we end up with a void, just nothingness. But that's not how being is. In a state of being, there is awareness, concentration, and clarity of mind—but not obsessive worry, the rehearsal of upcoming events, or the pensive mental processing that most of us regard as normal thinking.

When one is simply being, consciousness is focused on the here-and-now, not the there-and-then. The mind is not blank, but drinks in what the senses experience. There may be physical movement, even play, but it is not task-oriented motion. Whatever is done is done for its own sake, not as a means toward some other end, not to have something. When we are comfortable with "just being," then we are valuing ourselves intrinsically, separate from any of our prescribed social and economic roles. We no longer have to prove our worth, because just being is proof enough.

Animals are good at teaching humans about the experience of being. The lion sitting languidly beneath a shade tree, a puppy chasing its tail, the spider still and patient in its web, the hawk gliding high on a thermal, the bunny nestled in the grass beneath a gentle rain, the turtle sunning itself on a fallen log—all are creatures in a state of being. Certainly, all animals spend plenty of time and energy engaged in doing and having. The lioness hunts so she and the pride may survive, the puppy cleans itself, the spider tends its eggs and dispatches its prey, the bunny burrows a new warren. But, unlike many members of our species, animals take time to just be, to let go of doing and having so they can languish in the timeless, peaceful embrace of life's milieu.

"Animals know how to crawl back into the Earth's womb and allow the life force to nurture their souls," a naturalist friend told me.

When the otter cavorts in the stream, the family cat lounges half-awake in the summer grass, the manta ray settles into the silty bottom, the bat hangs inverted in its cave, or the doe idles in a cool thicket, each is resting in the arms of our Mother. At such times, creatures listen to the Earth's voice in the cascading stream or the crickets call, feel her breath in the wind, sense her movements in the passing shadows and bending trees, feel her touches in the soil and plants, rocks and water, smell her scents, and taste her flavors. Each sits waist-deep in life's warm, fertile pool, just soaking.

For many human animals the art of being is long forgotten. We have buried this gentle pastime beneath dense and furtive layers of activity and acquisition, imagining that getting things done and having nifty stuff will deliver peace of mind. But peace of mind is not made from pieces of stuff. And while there is an element of satisfaction in accomplishing tasks and having playthings, inner peace comes from doing nothing at all, and doing it well.

Many, perhaps most, of my clients would benefit from more being and less doing and having. Hoping to further this, I suggest to many that they practice the old art of sitting in some outdoor place and watching nature. "Contemplating life" is the term I use, because life *can* be contemplated. Television, traffic, football, Nintendo, computer monitors . . . these things are watched, not contemplated. Except in spectacular moments, nature does not demand our attention. It invites. It doesn't seek to control what we experience, as most electronic media do, but, rather, encourages us to dabble our senses and awareness in its infinite variety.

Contemplating animals and other life forms is best done some distance from human structures and activity, although even one's backyard can suffice. Just looking out my office window at the hawks rejuvenated my spirit. As anyone who has meandered about in the woods, prairie, mountains, or desert can attest, when we sit quietly there, our brethren creatures begin to appear. Birds commence their calls, squirrels and other small furry ones make their rounds, even deer, foxes, coyotes, and other larger mammals cross one's line of sight. If we take the time to look closely, insects provide fascinating viewing as well. Of course, some of them find us first.

As all good role models do, animals teach us about the art of being through example, not by lecture. If we watch them sufficiently, they demonstrate a balanced rhythm between task-oriented activity (doing and having), on the one hand, and just lying around or playing (being), on the other. While some creatures are tireless workers, many fit into their daily schedules sizable intervals of just-hanging-out, a strategy that contrasts sharply with the average human itinerary.

What's more, most animals other than ourselves operate on a schedule that is structured around the Earth's rhythms and cycles. By removing ourselves from the natural world, and surrounding ourselves with hermetically sealed homes with central heating and cooling, outdoor lighting, 24-hour food stores, shift work, and other nifty modern innovations, we have pushed aside the Earth's biological tempos. We no longer eat when we are hungry, but when our clocks or social conventions say so. We awaken to alarms, or to our late night worries, rather than living by a cadence based upon the sun and the seasons. For most, our only time in darkness is when we sleep. During the rest of our existence, we manufacture artificial day with electricity. The average American spends over 90 percent of her or his time indoors, cut off from nature's tempos.

Without these contrived environmental controls, animals are in synch with how the Earth runs her schedule. And, as a little observation will illustrate, nature leaves plenty of time for just fooling around. We don't.

Owners of animal "pets," as we call these companions, understand the soothing quality of contact with our brethren creatures. Dogs and cats, in particular, by their example encourage people to make the psychological shift into a state of being. Their immersion in the here-and-now draws out the human capacity for simply being. Even watching aquarium fish reduces stress and lowers blood pressure.

And while the necessities of our lives don't permit most of us to "just be" as much as sound mental health would require, one of the easiest ways to make room for being is by visiting our brethren creatures. We cannot be like them, but we can be with them. Their very presence can slow our desperate galloping, can quiet the voices in our heads urging more activity in less time, and can invite us to dwell for a little, wonderful while in the healing ambiance of nature.

After all, that's what family is for.

Just being.

CONVERSATION

*Did you know that trees talk? Well they do. They talk
to each other, and they'll talk to you if you listen.
Trouble is, white people don't listen. They never
learned to listen to the Indians, so I don't suppose they'll
listen to other voices in nature. But I have learned a lot
from trees: sometimes about the weather, sometimes
about animals, sometimes about the Great Spirit.*

Native American Walking Buffalo

We rounded a blind corner on the narrow
escarpment, grunting quietly under the load of 50-
pound packs. A broad alpine meadow of south
Yellowstone Park opened below us, with Heart Lake
shining in its middle like the prophetic jewel in the lotus
flower. Dennis, who was at the lead, stopped to soak in
the view, and Mort and I crunched to a halt behind him,
happy for the rest and the panorama. Suddenly, Mort bellowed out:
  "Full many a glorious morning have I seen
  Flatter the mountain tops with sovereign eye,
  Kissing with golden face the meadows green,
  Gilding pale streams with heavenly alchemy . . . "
Dennis and I listened, fascinated, amused and entranced all in one.
Mort's rendition of this Shakespearean sonnet blended perfectly with
the remainder of our experience—with the thin, clean air blowing up
the rocky facing, the sun in blunted luminescence behind some high
cirrostratus, the greens and dry yellows of the valley dotted with clus-
ters of trees and massive boulders, and the white and blue reflection

of the distant lake, our destination. His words articulated the expansive wonder in our hearts, and the joy of our good fortune to be alive at such a moment in such a place.

At intervals throughout the remainder of our five-day, back country trek, Mort bellowed out lines of poetry and verse, some of his own making, others from great and gifted writers inspired by the Earth's majesty. Dennis and I, young men in our early 20s, relished these recitations from our 65-year-old companion, a relative stranger we had met at the trailhead on the day of our departure and invited to tag along.

Our third day out, huddled about the campfire that pushed back the utter blackness of a cloudy night, I finally indulged my curiosity.

"Mort, what triggers your recitations?" I asked.

He scratched his bald head and then rubbed his scruffy whiskers. The glow of the fire reflected in his eyes.

"It's just my side of the conversation," he replied. "You see, the Earth speaks to me, and when she does, I speak back."

"Speaks to you?" Dennis asked.

"Oh, not with words, of course. The Earth is much too elegant to rely upon human vocabulary. Sometimes she talks to me in a gust of wind, or when an animal comes close by, or by showing me a new view, like that look we got of Heart Lake the other morning," he explained.

"So the poetry is your way of talking back?"

"Right. Poetry and music and painting are all ways we can speak back to the Earth in a language close to her own. I can't paint or carry a tune, so I recite poetry and verse," he continued, laughing kindly at himself.

The Earth talks, but even those who listen to her seem uncertain how to reply. The conversation is often one-sided. This came clear to me a few years ago when my best friend, Todd, and I drifted at anchor in his sailboat at 3 a.m. beneath the brightest full moon I've ever beheld. A soft, warm breeze ruffled the water like a mother's hand on a young child's head, lapping it lightly against the hull, swinging the boat slowly in the tree-lined bay. It was too wondrous a night to be missed in sleep, so we reclined in the cockpit, absorbing the quiet and beauty.

Coming out from the shadowed trees on the shore, out from the radiant luminescence of the white orb in the night sky, and riding on the breath-warm wind, I "heard" the voice of the Earth, the soft speaking to which Mort had referred years and miles before in the mountains. I remembered how that same voice had whispered to my soul countless times before in raging blizzards, in the silent drop of a dying leaf, in waters rampaging down a tortured cliff in free fall to the sea, and in the shimmer of the cottonwood's dance.

In all those times, and many others, I never knew how to reply. Like a mute, I could hear but not speak. When I tried, my own words sounded too foolish to my neurotic, self-conscious mind, and I had never been one to memorize poetry or verse, like Mort. But on that moonlit night on the water, somehow, I found another voice, one from my heart and not my head. It emerged as a sound rather than a voice, and was closer to music than words. I suppose it sounded like a chant, but it lacked order and repetition. It ascended from some deep place inside that I had never felt before, and rose like a baby's hand reaching for the face of its mother. And then, like the baby's hand, my "speaking" seemed to touch her, to merge with her voice out there on the wind and water, in the dark woods, and shining from the moon.

The Earth and I had a conversation.

As a good friend will do, Todd let me be. He never asked me to explain.

Two decades after I was blessed by hearing Mort's narrations and a few years past that night on the lake, my good friend Mike and I stood atop a towering bluff above the confluence of the Wisconsin and Mississippi rivers. A warm, windless but wet day left the park empty of humans except for ourselves, so the Earth's sounds were acute and uninterrupted. It was an excellent opportunity to have a conversation with her.

A songbird I'd never before heard called out from an oak a few throws to our left, and then another, its mate we presumed, echoed in reply. Taking care not to disturb their chatter, Mike and I exchanged silent glances, smiling in the recognition that we were being "talked to." After some time, the two winged ones fell silent long enough for Mike to emit his own response. A self-taught but respectable bird and animal caller, Mike did a creditable rendition of their melodious sounds, and, shortly, the three of them were conversing. The literal meaning of this discourse remained a mystery to Mike and me, but the deeper sense of it did not.

"What's the appeal?" I later asked Mike. "What makes you want to do animal calls?"

He thought about that awhile, twirling a jay feather between his index finger and thumb, and then a smile rippled his countenance.

"It feels basic, almost primeval. It's a kind of language that doesn't get tangled up in meaning and interpretation and all that cerebral stuff. Instead, it's more like music. It's the sort of communication that you don't think. Instead, you feel it," he said.

Many indigenous peoples regarded conversations with the Earth, either as a whole or through its many life forms and elements, as a basic aspect of their spiritual and social lives. They experienced being "talked to" by the rivers, mountains, animals, trees, and birds, and they developed individual and group rituals that facilitated two-way communication. In dances, chants, songs, and ceremonies, they transmitted their replies.

When I proselytize to folks about getting to know our Earth Mother, many have difficulty conceiving of their interactions with her as a true relationship. In their own thinking, they tend to confine relationships to exchanges between persons, or between persons and certain animals—primarily pets.

But to have a relationship with the Earth?

We all do. And where there is a relationship, there resides the possibility of a heartfelt conversation. The question is whether we intend to consciously cultivate this interaction or let it occur outside of our awareness. Those of us who have never learned to speak with the Earth, and, even worse, those who fail to hear her, suffer a kind of sensory deficit, an absence of sensitivity to the most vital of connections, that of species to planet, of child to Mother. This need not be so. We don't have to be environmental activists, geologists, Greenpeace warriors, shamans, or plant biologists to perceive the Earth's speaking. Her sensory languages are so diverse that there are sufficient "dialects" to reach everyone, but one must be a good listener. As in human relationships, the absence of interest and listening skills will impede the ability to truly hear.

People who want to converse with the Earth can begin with the easiest and most obvious avenue, by listening to her sounds. Wind in the trees, water over rocks, birds, rain, crickets, and countless other resonances are her speech. A little contemplation will reveal endless variations in tone, volume, tempo, timbre, and the other qualities of her voice. Like us humans, she sings melodiously, screams, whispers, shouts in joy, rants in rage, chants, and laughs. She doesn't lecture, however.

Then, if one has the courage to feel and look a tad foolish by social standards, one can reply by approximating her voice, just as Mike does the birds and animals with whom he speaks. I have sent angry, resentful clients out to scream back at the Earth during storms and raging tempests when she is screaming at us. I have encouraged others to whisper their secrets in reply to her own when she rustles tall grass with her breezes or trickles water in a tiny brook. Some have learned to sing her songs in bird calls, to bellow their joy in response to the vociferous crashing of her waves and surf, and to weep and wail in tandem with her winter winds and soaking rains.

These are not idle conversations. Within them, we meet our Mother, finding in her voice the clarity and richness of our own heart's speaking.

"The Earth hears me," Mort told us the last night out. All around us in the mountain canyon where we camped just below the Great Divide, the wind howled, as if affirming his assertion.

"How do you know?" Dennis asked, ever skeptical.

Mort smiled with that warm certainty that requires no defense and no explanation, and which holds no rancor toward those who doubt.

"The same way you know anything that matters in this world . . . in your heart," he replied.

I recall a man I sent into a November gale to rail against life, which he felt had cheated him and robbed him of his hopes and dreams. He had a bone to pick with life, and on that screeching cold day, nature seemed to have one to pick with him. He stood face forward into the buffeting blow, screaming his bitter resentments until he was emotionally spent, and had had his full say and then some.

"I never could have done that with a person, not even with you," he told me later.

"What was different about doing it with the Earth?" I asked.

"I felt safe. Everything I said and all the anger I said it with just got absorbed and carried away in that wind," he replied, and then smiled a little.

"What else?" I encouraged him to speak his thought.

"Well, it was like that wind and I were on the same wavelength. It was just as ticked off as I was. We understood each other. That made it easier. That made me feel like I wasn't alone," he explained.

"You weren't alone," I assured him.

The Earth doesn't just talk . . . she listens. What she has to say to us, and what we have to say to her, probably won't feed anybody's appetite for intellectual analysis. This "language" defies all the rational approaches to "talk therapy" that any teacher ever tried to instruct me with, but it constitutes a bona fide emotional discourse. Conversations with nature are honest, expressive, and alive, which is more than one can say about many human discussions.

So, if you want someone to talk with, and all those human ears and mouths seem not quite right for what you have to say and need to hear, consider having a heart-to-heart with the Earth.

She speaks your spirit's language.

EXERCISE:

CEREMONY OF CONVERSATION

Developing a dialogue with our Earth requires that we discern her language, learn some of its elements, and then speak with her. It is easier, I suspect, than learning a foreign language. We already know it deep in our spirits. Here is a ceremony for creating a conversation with the Earth.

- Go to a place that is rich with nature's language. I have found this in as common an environment as my back yard, so you need not hike into the wilds, or even leave the proverbial suburban lot. Her "speaking" may be heard in the wind, the songs of birds, crickets, falling rain or snow, a brook, a lake or seashore, in rustling leaves, or the calls of creatures.
- Spend some time (well spent, I will add) studying the Earth's voice in whatever form it comes to you. There is much to be discerned in her speaking—volume, tone, tempo, timbre, variation, repetition, and so forth. Truly and deeply listen to her voice, as you would a song that draws you in.
- Once you feel you have learned some of her language, create a way to "speak back" that approximates or harmonizes with her voice. Children, for instance, often try to mimic the sound of the wind when playing or telling stories. You may wish to sing or hum with the wind, as one example. If so, this is more than mimicry. It is dialogue.
- If you find your own voice insufficient for your purposes, consider using a musical instrument or other sound-making object to assist in your conversation with the Earth. Examples from some of my clients include playing chimes in harmony with a babbling brook, using cymbals or a drum to speak with a thunderstorm, and rubbing stones together to blend with the chirping of crickets, playing a flute to sing with the birds and using a rain stick to, of course, talk with the rain.

The possibilities appear quite literally endless and are limited only by the strictures of our imaginations and self-consciousness.

- Consider meditating for a few moments after a dialogue with the Earth, perhaps as a way of concluding the conversation by listening. Maybe our Mother will have something else to say to you.
- At the conclusion of a conversation, I encourage you to express your appreciation in whatever way feels most comfortable and sincere.

We talk a great deal, we humans, and often we imagine that what we have to say is eminently interesting and important. Hubris is alive and well in our species. I suspect Mother Earth has equally meaningful things to say to us, and we to her. The little time necessary to further this dialogue is well worth the effort.

A CHANGE OF WORLDS

What is life? It is the flash of a firefly in the night. It is the breath of a buffalo in the winter time. It is the little shadow which runs across the grass and loses itself in the sunset.

Crowfoot of the Blackfoot Nation

There is no destination . . . not even death.

If there is any existential certainty that seeps into the soul after the bond with the Earth has been brought into one's daily awareness, it is the timeless dimension of the life force, of which each of us is a manifestation. And in this certainty there is emancipation from fear.

This deliverance comes from comprehending in a heartfelt way that we are part of a vibrant process that has far preceded our individual existence, and that will long follow the demise of each of us as an organism. However, if we do not feel the bond with the natural order, then there is no solace in this notion, for it remains merely an abstract, airy idea.

"Sure, I realize life goes on and all that, but in the final analysis, I still die," one fellow told me, spitting cynicism and fear.

Concepts do not quiet the fear of death. They only muzzle it. One must *feel* the attachment with the life force—not just *think* the attachment—before there is peace of mind about one's biological expiration.

Ours has been dubbed "the age of anxiety." Many of us are chronically fearful, some in a low-grade, background sort of way, and others

131

in a full-bore, run-screaming-into-the-night panic. Again, alienation has been fingered as the culprit, though it's most often framed in terms of estrangement from parents, family, community, and self. If we had sufficient social and familial supports, we are told, we would be less fearful. Some fears would be soothed by these supports, but the dread of death is too deep to be quieted by good friends, an understanding family, or singing in the church choir.

Philosophers and psychologists call this persistent dismay and apprehension "angst." When we grope for the floor of our existence and feel nothing there, when we seem adrift without direction or control and have little hope of making shore, when life seems just a meaningless exercise in passing time that concludes with dissolution and oblivion, then we experience angst. At a basic level of human pathos, angst is the homeless child—alone, abandoned, and scared witless.

Those of us with angst experience an ever-present, though often unconscious, awareness of personal mortality. This dark shadow hovers in the back of our minds, waiting to step forward and place its hand on our shoulders, not just at the moment of death, but again and again across a lifetime. The fear of death is the most basic and overpowering of all our terrors, and it fuels many of the smaller anxieties and worries that rob us of peace of mind and the capacity to enjoy the time we possess.

Those of us who are afraid to die are also truly afraid to live, for living fully always engenders risks. To attempt to live without risk, without accepting the reality of death, is a struggle one cannot win. Many try, but they pay dearly for their efforts. Their existence is crowded with worries, control madness, obsessive concern about life's dangers, vague but painful anxieties, nameless fears, and persistent attempts to foretell the future and so control it. Such folks are constantly maneuvering to outwit what they perceive as the capricious whims of fate, and to sidestep the grim reaper. But his swath is too wide and too certain.

Just as we run from the rain, so we run from death. Just as we see the natural world as foreign, as an enemy, so we see death as a monstrous villain. Death is the great engine of change in the Earth's domain, so when we experience her as a stranger, death seems all the more sinister and ominous. For those who are alienated from the Earth, life and death seem partners in some macabre conspiracy to tantalize us with pleasures, joys, and dreams, only to whisk them away without warning or fairness. "Life's a bitch and then you die," is the anthem of this dour philosophy.

But to the person who is bonded with the Earth, "Life is school and then you graduate." We are here to learn, to experience, and to grow, and then to return to that from which we sprang—life. As an ecologist friend of mine puts it, "Death is Mother Earth's way of recycling."

As the great sages have long insisted, death and life are of the same fabric. They make each other possible. As Chief Seattle so aptly put it, "There is no death . . . only a change of worlds." This is not a lofty

132

philosophical notion, but an existent reality. It is the reality of the Earth, of the life force. When that force feels foreign to your soul, so does death. It becomes the designated enemy, though clearly it is not.

The enemy is not death—it is alienation from the life force. Alienation breeds inhumanity toward our fellow people and creatures, and toward the Earth itself. The enemy emerges when our awareness becomes dead to the life force, both in ourselves and in the rest of creation. More of us are robbed of a full life by alienation, cruelty, and ignorance than by death itself.

It is ironic that those who struggle most to prolong their individual existences are often the same people who are estranged from the Earth, who feel frightened, alienated, and victimized by the life force. They are so consumed attempting to prolong life that they never experience what they are striving to have more of.

When we accept ourselves as part of the natural world, then we understand that we do not die any more than it does. But if we feel ourselves as islands, as separate individuals who are disconnected from the natural world and strangers in its midst, then death is our gravest adversary and our deepest fear.

Living in fear is a tough way to transit one's time.

Mr. Cavanaugh, my godfather and the man who propelled me on my search for my real Mother, died after a full and joyful life. The last time I saw him alive, he was still in reasonably good health, and there was little indication, at least to me, that his passing was close at hand. I walked him out to his car at the conclusion of a party at my parents' home, and as we were about to part, he paused for what would be our final good-bye.

"Phil," he said as he looked me straight in the eyes, as was his custom. "I figure you're about the best friend I've got."

I was a little embarrassed by his affection, being at that time a young man who was striving to create the persona of adult maturity and sophistication, but there was an intensity to his words and manner.

"Thanks," I replied, my unease slipping away. "I've always felt like you were mine, too."

He smiled and squeezed my arms with his still strong but old, bony hands. Then he was gone.

And so shall we all be.

But gone where?

If the Earth is not truly alive as a conscious and wise entity, if it is not actually our Mother in the real sense of that title, if it is just an organic factory, merely a biological experiment operating off a cosmic CPU, and we are only lab animals in some carbon-based procedure, then death is not a passage or a new beginning. It is the end. Oblivion.

Each of us grapples with this question. Is there life after death?

While there is no factual answer to this mystery, there is a heartfelt one. I worked for many years as a counselor in a hospital's oncology (cancer) unit, later in a community-based hospice program for the terminally ill, and more recently with dying people in my private

133

practice. Hundreds of times I have looked into the eyes of those just about to step into that shadowy passage that pulls us away from this life. I have come to know the look of fear and that of comfort on their faces.

Over these years and relationships, I have discerned a fundamental distinction between those who walk up to death's door with cold terror rattling in their hearts, and those who slip through with certainty in their souls. The latter often seem grounded in the Earth. In their final days they speak to me of nature's beauties, of times spent among the Earth's wonders, of adventures in the wild, of childhoods spent in woods, on lakes, and on mountains, and of gardening, farming, fishing, milking cows, and climbing trees (and falling out of them). And they talk of those they loved, and of their capacity to honor other life—not just family and friends, but pets, trees, and gardens.

"Want to know the four most important things in my life?" a man in his 60s and dying of cancer asked me.

"Sure do," I replied.

"My wife, my daughter, my son, and my vegetable garden," he laughed and cried simultaneously.

"Sounds about right." I put a hand on his forearm.

"The garden part usually takes people back a little," he continued. "But all that growing and working the soil made me feel a part of life, if you know what I mean."

"Believe me, I understand," I reassured him.

And there was the terminally ill woman, a mother of six, who ran a tree nursery with her husband for over 30 years.

"I've watched a lot of things grow and a lot of things die," she told me.

"What do you make of all that growing and dying?" I asked.

"Death doesn't stop life one bit. Life just keeps coming. There's something in the Earth that just won't quit," she replied.

"And what about you?"

"I feel like there's something in me that just won't quit either," she concluded.

And there is. The life force that drives our cells, fires our synapses, moves our lungs and hearts and limbs, flashes in our eyes, and ripples in our laughter and tears, does not come from within us. It comes through us. It comes from the Earth, from our Mother, from the same goddess that gave us existence. And it does not go with us; it does not disappear with our demise as organisms. It lives on, somehow, somewhere, in some way that nobody quite understands. Those of us who know our Mother feel this truth to the very bottom of our hearts.

As Thomas Binney, an English theologian from the 19th century said, "She (nature) undergoes change, but there's no annihilation—the essence remains."

We were born from nature, and we die back into her.

Like raindrops pulled up from the sea and then rained back, over and over, our lives move in unbroken circles.

Eternal.

GRATITUDE

When I was ten years of age, I looked at the land and the rivers, the sky above, and the animals around me and could not fail to realize that they were made by some great power. I was so anxious to understand this power that I questioned the trees and the bushes. It seemed as though the flowers were staring at me, and I wanted to ask them, "Who made you?" I looked at the moss-covered stones; some of them seemed to have the features of a man, but they could not answer me. Then I had a dream, and in my dream one of these small round stones appeared to me and told me that the maker of all was Wakan Tanka (Great Spirit), and that in order to honor him I must honor his works in nature.

Native American Brave Buffalo

While in the woods, I enjoy stalking.

Not just wild animals, which I don't hunt but delight in getting close to, but also humans. Most folks are noisy when they're out in the wild, which is why they rarely encounter other animals.

One afternoon while off the beaten path in an Iowa state park that held magnificent stands of old oak, I heard someone thrashing about in some nearby brush. Circling in quietly, I soon spotted an older, bearded fellow wearing gardener's gloves and a broad-brimmed hat, with a canvas bag strung over his neck and one shoulder. As he struggled through the thick bushes, he never looked up or around, but kept his gaze sweeping back and forth across the ground.

I elected to make my presence known.

"Hello there," I called, stepping from behind a large tree.

135

"Howdy," he hailed back, smiling as he wiped sweat from his brow.
"A fine day, and a fine woods," I said.

"Yes, indeed. I truly admire this forest, and I come here often," he replied.

We shook hands and exchanged names and other pleasantries before I got around to indulging my curiosities.

"What's in your sack?" I asked.

His friendly smile soured, and a pained sadness spilled into his eyes.

"Litter," he answered. "I come here once a month or so to pick up trash. Find all sorts of stuff. Beer cans, of course, and plastic bags, Styrofoam cups, cigarette butts, old shirts and socks, newspaper, broken glass . . . just about anything you can imagine."

"Sad," I muttered.

"Yes. Hell, once I found a whole case of cosmetics. I can't figure how *that* got out here." He laughed sadly.

We both stared around at the sun-soaked woods for a moment, silently sharing a deep regret that some people violate so sacred a place without the slightest hesitation or remorse. The trees bent over in the humid wind, as if they were sighing along with us.

"Why do you do it?" I asked.

His countenance softened more, and I saw the edges of tears catch on the rims of his eyes. He fought them back with considerable effort.

"Well," he began, looking up at the trees towering over us, "I figure I owe it."

"Owe it? To whom?"

"To life . . . to Mother Earth."

Then I strained to hold back my own tears.

One of the hallmarks of a healthy mind and spirit is gratitude, an earnest thankfulness for the gifts one has been given in life; indeed, for the gift of life itself. Sadly, gratitude is absent in many of us today. In its place we find an egocentric sense of entitlement, as if life owes us instead of the other way around.

The illusion of entitlement doesn't stem from wealth and privilege alone. It also stems from our fundamental estrangement from the natural world. This missing attitude (gratitude) has propelled the pursuit of wealth and power at any price, and particularly at the expense of the biosphere. It has fueled the pollution, littering, and degradation of our planet that now threatens the very existence of our species and of many others, and which has already degraded our emotional and spiritual health.

Those who feel bonded with and grateful to our Earth Mother don't dump barrels of toxic waste in rivers, don't throw empty cans and bottles from their cars, don't clear-cut forests, drain wetlands, or shoot bald eagles. Their relationship with the natural world is one of reverence. They consider the life force and its manifestations sacred, and feel duty bound to "give back" because they have received so much.

They have been honored by their Mother, and they honor her in return.

A PLACE CALLED HOME

*The natural world is a spiritual house . . . . Man walks
there through forests of physical things that are also
spiritual things, that watch him with affectionate looks.*

Author Charles Baudelaire

It's been said that home is not a place, but rather
a feeling.

I have written this belief, in one fashion or another, throughout these pages. And while that assertion is
often correct, that home is a state of heart, not a location of body, it is also accurate that place can be an
important part of the experience of being home. Many of us
seek home beneath the roof of the house of our dreams, while
others feel it more in cars, or even at the office. If you ask most
folks where they feel "at home," house, car, or workplace are the
primary contenders.

My own place called home has moved around over the years.
Presently, it sits atop a moraine in southern Wisconsin. There are
no houses there, no human structures of any kind—just a
grassy, flower-strewn prairie overlooking a broad valley.
Fortunately, someone had the foresight to set this locale aside for the
sort of home-making I so sorely require to sustain my sanity. It was an
old farm, but it is now a nature center.

I go home often, at all times of day or night, and throughout the
seasons of the year. It's never crowded there, although I happen upon

other home-seekers on occasion. Gradually, I've discovered those times of the day and year when people are least likely to be in the vicinity, and my visits cluster around these intervals of solitude.

Despite the relative absence of people, my home is not lonely or somber. In fact, it is quite crowded with life. Multitudes of plants and animals live in and frequent this home, and birds visit often. The sky is close, as well. The hill seems to push me up to it, making the sun, moon, and clouds closer somehow. There is always music—the wind in the grass, the crickets, the snow sifting through the dry stems, the rumble of distant thunder, or the shimmer of rain. And the aromas are as inviting as fresh bread baking in the oven. Accommodations for sitting or lying are Spartan by modern standards, but the feel is real.

But the most wondrous aspect of my home is the feeling that comes to me when I am there. In that place, I hear, see, feel, smell, and touch the Earth with an uncommon intensity. For whatever reason—one I do not pretend to comprehend—that particular place makes her real and present for me, more so than any other. I know that when I go there, the Earth Mother will be there for me, no matter the weather, the season, or my state of mind.

In that, there is profound comfort and steadfast sanity.

This home, this place where our Mother is present for me, will shift again some day, as it has many times in the past. I don't understand why these shifts occur, but I know that they do, and I have come to expect them. When they happen, I get a sense of being pulled to something new and of being taken on a journey of change. It may have something to do with learning, as most of life does, but I'm not certain.

When this strong sense of the Earth leaves the place that feels like home for me, I go looking for her presence and my new home. This search is delicious in its own way. It draws me to new spaces—deep forests, glens, rivers, hills, rock cuts, old quarries, wind-swept prairies, cedar bogs, parks, orchards, ponds, farm fields, beaches, gardens—anywhere that is more about the Earth and less about human habitation. It becomes a quest. Not only do I discover new and beautiful locales, but also I discern new ways of perceiving our Earth Mother. She has so many ways of showing herself. And each time, at least so far, I find her again. She lets me.

It's so reassuring to find home again and to feel welcome there.

As you've likely guessed, I persuade many of my clients to go "home hunting," as well. Those who are starkly alienated from the Earth to begin with have a rough time of it. Often, they never discover that sense of home in any place, outdoors or indoors. They return to me, questioning why I shooed them off to stumble among the brambles, bugs, and snowdrifts seeking some spiritual connection with this invisible goddess, whom they suspect I fabricated in my zanier moments.

But others are surprised, even shocked, to discover their spiritual home in some unlikely corner of the natural world, in some place of no particular note or attraction save for its proclivity for enveloping their hearts in the glowing certainty of belonging. These fortunate ones learn the meaning of the word "sacred." For that is what a home with our Mother is—a sacred place. In such a place, we feel the spiritual umbilical that binds each of us with the Earth that bore us. There, one remembers. The who, why, and where of existence slip into place like puzzle pieces—once so perplexing but suddenly so simple. There, nature's way is revealed. Healing begins.

I don't know why one place is sacred for one person and not for another, or why one's home in nature may move about unpredictably at times. These are mysteries in the truest sense of that word. The ancients, tribal peoples, even children today, all knew and know of such places. They did not wonder why, although most of us adult, modern folk will. Too often it is our custom to slice and dice everything, particularly a mystery.

But I do know that home is there. Healing is there. It is made of sky and wind, clouds and storms, trees and berries, creatures of wondrous variety, soil and rock, vistas and valleys, water and air, and things dying and being born. It is a place where the earth reaches out to each of us with a touch that we remember, somehow, from an unremembered time.

The touch of life.

The way of healing.

Go home.

EPILOGUE

Nature and wisdom always say the same.

Roman Poet Juvenal

"What can I do?" a young mother asked after hearing me speak about the theme of this book.

"What do you want to grow?" I asked. Psychotherapists almost always answer a question with a question, an irritating occupational habit.

"I want to get back to that bond with the Earth, and I want my children to grow up feeling it, too. I want them to learn nature's way," she replied.

As far as life changes go, rediscovering one's covenant with nature is exceedingly simple. If you've ever tried to lose weight, stop smoking, change careers, improve your self-image, or stop worrying, you'll find bonding with the Earth as easy as falling off the proverbial log. In fact, falling off a log may help immensely, provided you stay put on the ground for awhile afterwards.

As is true of any relationship, some investment of time and energy is necessary, but communication with nature is often far less conflicted and confusing than interacting with humans. The Earth's messages are reasonably straightforward.

141

There are many ways to "go home" to nature. Some are almost too obvious to mention, but each time I do mention them I run into some of us who have overlooked the obvious. I think TV has a lot to do with our diminished consciousness about the obvious. Everything on TV is obvious, and we get bored and tranced-out accordingly.

Anyway, here are some simple steps for adults and children, in no particular order:

- Whenever possible, get your skin in touch with the air, soil, water, and vegetation. Walk barefoot on the soil. Dance in the rain and let it soak you. Plant your behind on the ground each day. Burrow into the snow long enough to let the clean cold wake up your organism. Dig around in the soil and sand (no gloves please). Swim. Better yet, if you can pull it off (so to speak), go skinny dipping. Go out on a windy day and let it blow your hair around. Lie face down in the grass or, better yet, in a prairie or on the beach.

- Hug your Mother. Wrap yourself around a tree, even if you aren't climbing it. Hold a big rock (you don't have to lift it) and feel how it has absorbed the hot or cold of the day. Make a snowman. Jump into a hay mound. Embrace a wave crashing on the beach.

- Wake up your senses through the natural world. Focus your tactile awareness on rocks, leaves, nuts, flowers, bark, feathers, seaweed, shells, sand, dirt, and anything else that won't bite or give you a rash. Smell the scents and listen to the sounds. If you know what you're doing with wild plants, taste them. If you don't know, taste nature via produce from an organic farmer. And use your eyes. The Earth's nuances and colors are not confined to blazing sunsets and full-bore autumn landscapes. Even the so-called drabness of winter is resplendent with subtle visual tone.

- Surround your indoor home or office with life, including plants, stones, feathers, acorns, pussy willow, dried "weeds" (I hate that term), and other natural items whose abduction from the outdoors will not damage the environment or detract from others' enjoyment of it. In displaying these items, consider a nature table for your home. A nature table is particularly helpful in sustaining the bond between the Earth Mother and young children, so place one in each of their rooms.

- Go home-hunting in nature. You don't need to be a seasoned backcountry hiker, whitewater canoeist, mountaineer, or cave-dwelling ascetic to meander about in parks, conservancy areas, state and national forests, or nearby fields, beaches, and woodlands in search of a place that feels sacred to you. Find a location in nature where you experience nature's presence clearly, and visit there often. Considering all the other places we frequent, a little time and travel to one's sacred space is well worth it.

- "Speak" to the Earth. I don't mean you have to talk to your house plants, though that's fine, too. Listen for her language, her dialects, and play with learning one or more of these natural tongues. Howl like a windstorm, crash and rumble like thunder, shush with the rain, learn to call with birds and animals, sing or chant with the ebb and flow of the surf, play a drum or other musical instrument in concert with one of nature's sounds. My seven-year-old daughter whistles with the wind using blades of grass. If you adults feel foolish or don't know how to get into this, have your kids show you. Play it as a game. They already know how. They'll teach you.

- Take a day each month and serve nature. Pick up litter, volunteer to help with a recycling program, assist with environmental education at your local nature center, participate in a Nature Conservancy campaign, or some other effort to give something back to the Earth that gave us life. This is helpful for the whole family, especially for young children who need to learn gratitude and service.
- Garden. There are few things that are more satisfying, both emotionally and spiritually. When you raise flowers or vegetables or fruit trees, you participate intimately with nature's workings, with the cycle of birth, life, death, and rebirth. Gardening *is* psychotherapy.
- Lobby your local school or your child's teacher to include environmental education (done outdoors, please) in the core curriculum. This should be hands-on, frequent, and based more on direct contact with nature than on electronic media. Volunteer to help out.
- Join an environmental group dedicated to preserving, honoring, and restoring the Earth's creative wonders. Contributing money is good and necessary, but direct involvement will feed your spirit and help crystallize your bond with the Earth.
- Petition your local government to allow and encourage "natural lawns." Yards full of native grasses and wildflowers don't require herbicides, pesticides, or frequent watering. They provide living "shrines" to our Earth Mother, attract wildlife and children, and embrace the life force's proclivity for diversity. There's nothing creative or diverse about a yard that looks like a golf course. Many municipalities and subdivisions have ordinances against natural lawns, or laws that prohibit grass beyond certain restrictive heights. Educate and organize your fellow citizens and bring them to their senses . . . quite literally. Imagine waking up each day to a tall grass or wildflower-strewn prairie instead of a lawn that needs mowing.
- Taking reasonable safety precautions, go out in storms. Very few of us get soaked in a hard rain, cavort in a wild wind, or brave a heavy snow. Storms are adventures, and enduring their adversity enlivens and strengthens one's spirit.
- Go animal watching. This is quite simple. Find a secluded area in nature away from human activity and just sit, listen, and watch. If you are quiet and blend in with your surroundings, animals and birds will soon appear and go about their business, paying you little or no heed. You can always count on the bugs,

except in winter, of course. Take some binoculars for close-ups.

- Boating is good, provided you leave the motor behind. A canoe or flat-bottomed rowboat will allow you to slip into shallow, secluded areas near shores on lakes and rivers. There you will find a wide array of plant, animal, insect, and bird life that will reveal itself if you are quiet.

These are but a few approaches to re-bonding with the Earth. Generally, they do not demand huge chunks of time or gut-busting effort; but whatever time or energy is required will be well worth the investment.

Rediscovering one's physical, emotional, and spiritual origins in the Earth is more than fun, uplifting, calming, enlightening, reassuring, and awe-inspiring.

It is right and true.

True to life.